EKCO's of Cowbridge
House and War Factory

by

Bob Browning

A catalogue record for this book is available from the
British Library.

ISBN 0-9551842-0-7

Published by Cowbridge Publishing
Cowbridge Cottage, Malmesbury,
Wiltshire SN16 9LZ, United Kingdom
+44 (0) 1666 823994

Cover designed by
David Forward

Typeset by
Sue Austin Business Support
48 St Dennis Road, Malmesbury, Wiltshire SN16 9BH

Printed and bound in Great Britain by
Antony Rowe Ltd
Bumper's Farm Industrial Estate, Bristol Road,
Chippenham, Wiltshire SN14 6LH

Contents

Acknowledgements

Bibliography

Introduction

Early Days

A Spanish Nobleman

A King's Yachtsman

The EKCO Factory

EKCO Works Social and Sports Club

Postcards

What Now?

Acknowledgements

I have been very lucky in this project; so many people have been generous with their time and memories. Dick Grainger a former Site Manager at the factory had fortunately rescued from being thrown out, relevant photos, scrapbooks, newspaper cuttings and sales catalogues. All of these he kindly loaned me. I contacted him, and several other former employees, through his secretary Mrs Frances Farmer who still had the minutes book from the Ekco Sports and Social Club.

I am grateful for the permission of the Trustees of the Mass-Observation Archives to reproduce material in this book.

The two maps shown are with kind permission of Ordnance Survey.

Thanks are due to the staff of the Wiltshire Museum and Library Service at Trowbridge.

A Bertodano family member loaned me not only his ancestor Baldomero's photograph album but glass photographic plates. The Hunloke family loaned me David Dixon's book on Sir Philip, The King's Sailing Master and helped with their family history. Then a direct descendant from Charles Kemble and Samuel Brooke allowed access to Kemble's own photographic collection - a treasure trove indeed.

Maureen Driver from the Minton Group without whom the two Open Days would not have been possible, kindly allowed me on site on numerous occasions. The security guards were always understanding and patient with me.

Terry Thomas has taken many of the present day photographs and has always been an encouragement. David Forward who designed the book cover, also allowed me to use material from his "Malmesbury Memories" web site.

Teresa de Bertodano has also been not only been a great encouragement but has corrected so much of my work. Any mistakes are entirely of my own making.

Without the constant support of Wendy my wife this venture could not have been completed, at a time when the roles should have been reversed.

Sue Austin has managed to untangle the threads of my efforts and weave them into an acceptable format.

So many townspeople have loaned me pictures and told stories of their time at Ekco, there must be lots more still to do; perhaps this will inspire someone else to build on my efforts.

Bibliography

War Factory. Celia Fremlin. Mass Observation, 1943

The Kings Sailing Master. Douglas Dixon. George G. Harrap. 1948

Andrews & Drurys *Map of Wiltshire*, Published by Wiltshire Archaeological & Natural History Society, 1773

The Postcard Century. Tom Phillips. Thames & Hudson, 2000

War Walks. Stop Line Green. Maj. Green. Reardon Publishing, 1999

Introduction

In 1970 I moved to Cowbridge Cottage on the main Swindon road about a mile from the Market Cross in the Wiltshire town of Malmesbury with my wife and two young daughters. At that time I knew nothing of the history of Cowbridge House, in fact I was barely aware of its existence.

Alongside our new home it was just possible to see a single storey brick building, almost hidden amongst the trees. We knew that we would be living next door to what was then a very busy factory. Our new neighbours, two elderly spinster sisters, told us that the factory was quiet and that we would not be troubled by its presence. Later conversations with the two Miss Simkins revealed that their family had arrived in Malmesbury with Sir Philip Hunloke when he bought the Cowbridge estate in the 1920s. They also explained that their late father, known to everyone as "Simmy", had been groom to Sir Philip and that our cottage had been the home of his gardener. Both sisters had at some time worked either in the house or on the estate. Intriguingly we were told that amongst the various newer buildings the old house was still standing.

Walking towards Cowbridge Farm immediately behind the factory, we obtained glimpses of what had been a good-sized Country House. I had moved to Malmesbury as a postman and was enjoying the secrets that that job unfolds, so I saw more of the house when delivering mail to the factory. In the early 1970s there was a posting box set into the wall outside the factory. Cowbridge had obviously been a house of some standing locally, the box has since been moved to Cowbridge Crescent and all that remains here is a short path in the grass leading to a blank stone wall!

Over thirty-five years since 1970 the factory has seen many changes, the workforce came and went, as did various owners. Many of the trees, which had hidden the wartime brick buildings so successfully, were taken down, and modern office blocks took their place. But Cowbridge House remained. I learned a little of its history, there was talk of "The King's Yachtsman", of a Royal Air Force pilot "Cats Eyes" Cunningham and of a Spanish nobleman. I was shown a postcard of the house and its wonderful Italianate garden. I was told it had been the birthplace of radar and that Queen Mary had visited during World War Two. I was told stories of "Simmy" the character who was the neighbour I never knew. When questioned as to where I lived, I learned to answer with "Next to the Ekco factory" Everyone in town then knew exactly where the new postman lived!

After the last owners, Lucent Technologies, sold the site and it had stood empty and desolate for a year or more we heard that a group of developers proposed to demolish Cowbridge House to build houses on the site. The Minton Group, the owners, kindly allowed Malmesbury Civic Trust to hold two Open Days on the factory site. There I heard wonderful recollections from previous employees, and of Hetty Wicks then a 90 year old revisiting for the first time the house where she was taken as a baby to visit the owners.

It was then that I decided to try and collect at least a few of the stories and memories of some of the people who had been connected with the house and the factory.

This book is an attempt to set down at least part of the history of this house, which has had a considerable influence and impact on the town of Malmesbury.

Early Days

The estate of Cowbridge lies about a mile South East of the Wiltshire town of Malmesbury at the edge of the Cotswolds. For years this has been dairy farming country, with the River Avon running through the valley.

Since the 1500s it has had a mill on site, which was at one time leased to William Stumpe the wealthy clothier. It was Stumpe who was responsible for turning the nave of Malmesbury Abbey into a workshop when the wool trade was so profitable. In 1615 Henry Grayle and his son David owned the mill and twenty acres.

For a large part of the seventeenth century the mill was leased to a clothing family from Calne named Foreman. The last reference to its use in the grinding of corn is in 1723 when the mill was available to let. At that time it contained two pairs of stocks for clothing, a dye house, a comb shop and a gristmill.

Cowbridge as it looked circa 1910, the bridge pictured was replaced in 1930 by the bridge we see today with far fewer arches
Postcard. Ron Peel Collection

On the maps of Wiltshire produced in 1773 by John Andrews and Andrew Dury Cow Mill House and its gardens make their appearance and were in the ownership of William Carey. Cow Mill House was a large house near to the mill itself. It is shown as one of only half a dozen houses in the area.

Cartographers included individual dwellings on their maps in the hope that wealthy owners would buy copies of the maps on which their houses appeared. The inclusion of Cow Mill House confirms the standing of the property at that time.

Samuel Bendry Brooke

I am uncertain as to when Cow Mill House became Cowbridge House.

Cowbridge takes its name from the bridge that carries the main Swindon Malmesbury road over the River Avon. Until very recently cows did indeed cross Cowbridge but sadly the last herd of milking cows has gone. Today we can still benefit from the work of the Victorian owners who planted the many trees around the estate. Approaching the House from Cowbridge farm drive we see behind the old buildings the bright green of beech trees bursting into leaf. There are copper beech trees alongside them, which are equally colourful. The bank side of the Swindon Road was originally planted with both red and white flowering horse chestnuts, some of which have sadly disappeared over the years. There is no longer any sign of the Monkey Puzzle tree that appears in early photographs. This is a tree without which no Victorian garden would have been complete. Over the years many other trees have been felled to make room for factory extensions.

By 1828 the Ordinance Survey map shows cottages on the Swindon Road. These had been built to house the staff employed in the house or on the estate. The tithe records from 1841 show the tenant as a Mr Henry Young who paid a tenth of his profits to the owner of Cowbridge House Samuel Bendry Brooke. The Brooke family were wealthy landowners and became wealthier as successful tea brokers. The family name lives on in Brooke Bond Tea. The Brooke family owned Cowbridge from the early 1700s.

Two of the pastures in early tithe records were named Little Rack Mead and Rack Hill; names long since forgotten.

Cowbridge House near Malmesbury. The seat of Samuel Bendry Brooke to whom this plate is inscribed with sentiments of the highest respect by his obliged servant John Shaw architect

Some Brooke and Kemble family members at the mill building at Cowbridge

The new Italianate gardens

In the 1850s Samuel Brooke had the house redesigned and rebuilt by the architect John Shaw. An elaborate Italianate garden was added to the south front. This had stone terraces, ornate flowerbeds, and two gravity fed fountains. To the rear were walled vegetable gardens with several greenhouses. This no doubt maintained Cowbridge's prestige alongside other country houses of a similar size.

Samuel Brooke is shown seated in the centre of the group wearing a stovepipe hat with Charles Kemble to his left and with the Reverend's mother Mrs C. A. Kemble seated to the Reverend's left

In 1857 Samuel Bendry Brooke and his sister Mrs C.A. Kemble financed the building of the Junior and Infants School in Malmesbury.

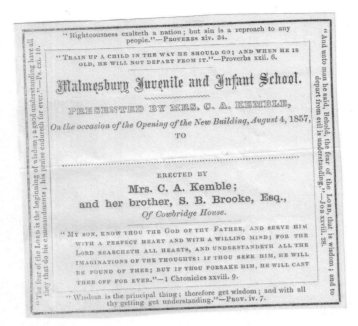

School opening notice

One of the earliest photos of Cowbridge: from Charles Kemble's photograph album c1875

The clock tower sadly now demolished

On Brooke's death in 1869 the house passed into the hands of his nephew the Reverend Charles Kemble. Mr Kemble also inherited Maunditts Park at Little Somerford, an estate at Braydon and Overtown Estate at Wroughton near Swindon. He became Rector of Bath Abbey and spent some of his wealth on its restoration during the late nineteenth century. There is a screen dedicated to his memory in the Abbey today. Kemble's family had owned Widhill farm and land at Blunsdon near Swindon since the 1400s. He also owned Vellore a large house in Bath, which is now the Royal Spa Hotel.

It is interesting to see in the metal work of the railings on a bridge over the millstream near the entrance to Cowbridge, the initials C. K. in two of the roundels.

Reverend Charles Kemble

Roundel in the metal work

The same initials appear on a large block of carved stone that is now in a Cotswold garden. It was originally part of a sundial base and was rescued in the early 1980s when work was in progress on the Cowbridge site. Some of the artefacts were being destroyed and a neighbour living close to Cowbridge found the carved stone attractive. Not wanting it to be destroyed, she kept it in her garden. When her children were small they climbed onto it for a better view of the area so it became known as "The nosey stone". It has now found a home in the Cotswold garden of a direct descendant of both Samuel Brooke and the Reverend Charles Kemble.

The nosey stone

The Kemble family crest is a boar's head, and the Brooke crest shows a brock or badger. On the base of the stone and in the roundels of the bridge appears an animal's head, which looks rather more wolf like.

Kemble's name lives on in a cul-de-sac of dwellings named after him off Cowbridge Crescent.

Certified by John Kemble.

The Kemble family coat of arms

Two of Charles Kemble's 12 children: Rachel born 1857 at Cowbridge and christened by her father at Bath Abbey and Jessie born, 1861 at Vellore Bath. Sitting in front with her sister is four-year-old Elizabeth-Ann Bubb, great great granddaughter of Charles Kemble and the owner of Kemble's sundial base, the Nosey Stone

The mid 1800s was an exciting time in the history of the town. For a number of years meetings had been held to decide the route of the forthcoming railway, which would connect Malmesbury to London by joining the main line at Dauntsey. The railway was to run beneath the main Malmesbury Swindon road within yards of Cowbridge House and there were plans at one stage for a halt at Cowbridge. Though in fact had it materialized it was to be known as Burton Hill Halt. This was no doubt because one of the main railway shareholders was Colonel Miles who lived at Burton Hill House!

Work was undertaken in the area that now belongs to Willis's Fencing Company to level the ground ready for a platform, but for some reason it never happened. When groundwork for the platform was undertaken in that area, a complaint was made by the Commanding Officer of the Rifle Brigade. The proposed platform would shorten their rifle range by several yards and he was not happy about it.

The line runs a few yards from Cowbridge millpond before curving away through Lea Fields towards the first sight of the Abbey and Malmesbury town. It is not hard to imagine the excitement that would have been generated by the first train to pass Cowbridge House in 1877. The sight of this attractive group of buildings must also have impressed the passengers. At one time as many as six trains a day would have passed the house.

A view of the estate looking across the railway line towards the millpond. The only remaining buildings are the mill house and Cowbridge House itself, which is seen amongst the trees on the left

The house was again offered for sale in 1894. A sales catalogue describes the River Avon at Cowbridge in glowing terms "This noted trout stream is itself one of the special features and viewed from the higher ground forms in the bright sunshine a beautiful silvery band, winding away in the valley of rich water meadows with the picturesquely timbered and undulating background in the distance. A combination of nature's charms which go to complete an ideal retreat for the angler.

Almost Matchless fishing ÿ trout up to 7lb, pike at 20lb, Chubb at 4lb and both perch and roach at 2lb each plus dace and tench of a good size can all be caught."

The catalogue tells the prospective purchaser that the mill has a 14-foot iron breast shot water wheel 10 inches wide, which might be used for an electricity supply. At this date the stables have gaslights. A social advantage listed was "A number of Gentleman's seats within easy distance".

A Spanish Nobleman

Kemble's son put the house up for sale and in 1899 it was bought by Baldomero Hyacinth de Bertodano, who was a partner in a firm of solicitors in the City of London. His own family were believed to have played their part in the reconquest of Spain from the Moors.

In the sixteenth century three successive generations of Bertodano's, then called Bertendana, had risen to eminence in the Spanish Navy. The eldest Martin commanded the ship which took the Emperor Charles V back to Spain after his abdication. The next, also Martin, commanded the ship which brought the Emperor's son Philip II to England to marry Mary Tudor. The third, another Martin, commanded the Levantine squadron in the ill-fated Spanish Armada, indeed he was the only leader whose professional career continued after the Armada's disastrous end.

Baldomero (known as Baldo) had inherited the Burrage estate in Woolwich from his mother's family when he was 51. Soon after he came to Malmesbury he became a very generous benefactor to the town. Although baptised into the Roman Catholic faith he attended services in the Church of England and provided the cost of the restoration of the Abbey parvis.

Baldo on the steps

Both Baldo and his brother Charles were high-ranking officials in a London Freemason's Lodge, the Pattison Lodge, so called after their mother's family, the Pattisons. The two brothers were the driving force behind the formation in Malmesbury of the Saint Aldhelm Lodge in 1902, which still flourishes today. At the consecration, lunch was taken in a marquee in the grounds of the Bell Hotel, morning dress and silk hats were to be worn. This was followed by a ceremony at the Town Hall and a Service at the Abbey. Baldomero designed a Founder's jewel after considerable research at the British Museum about the arms of Malmesbury Abbey and the seal of the Abbot. Amongst the professions of the first lodge members were a hay and cattle dealer, a forage contractor, a veterinary surgeon and a wine merchant. Both Bertodano brothers wrote down as their profession "Gentleman".

The two brothers donated both the furnishings and the sashes and the ladies of the Brethren including Baldo's four sisters made the original Lodge banner. He and his brother were also great supporters of the Malmesbury Boy Scout group. Whenever the group went off to camp a hamper of fruit and vegetables accompanied it from the kitchen gardens at Cowbridge.

The kitchen gardens

15

Just some of the many greenhouses

Gable end of the chauffeur's lodge

Baldo enjoyed the role of Edwardian Country Gentleman, having inherited through his Spanish forebears the title Marques del Moral which he fancied entitled him to have a coronet on the side of his Rolls Royce. It was suggested to him by Lord Carnwath (whose daughter had married Baldo's nephew) that this was rather vulgar; his answer shows a very practical side to the man: "Possibly, but it does help me get through the traffic."

Close to the chauffeur's lodge and garage, which bears the date 1910, amongst the trees at Cowbridge is what appears to be an Oriental pagoda.

Baldo's ornate petrol store

The motorcar was not used on all occasions

The consecration of the war memorial

Ordnance Survey 1900

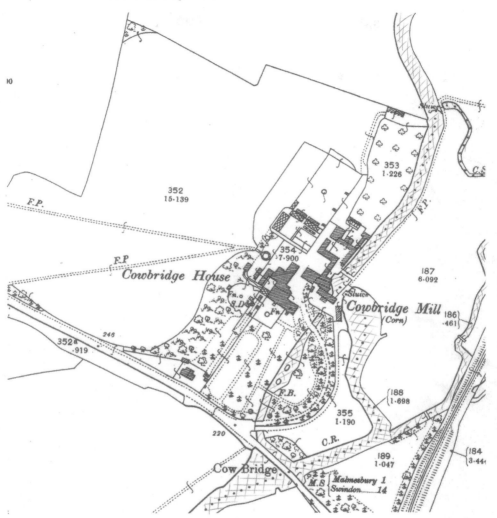

Note the changes in the two maps. Cowbridge farm has been built by 1921. Extra greenhouses show and many more trees have been planted including an avenue in the parkland. A reservoir shows where Cowbridge Crescent now is and a posting box appears in the wall on the main road.

Ordnance Survey 1921

At the turn of the century there were very few roadside garages to supply petrol, there was simply no need of them as there were not many people with cars. The pagoda is in fact Baldo's highly decorative and private petrol store. He was a competent carpenter and he and his brother may well have been the craftsmen responsible for some of the carvings in the billiard room and the beam ends in the main hall.

At the end of the First World War there was a public subscription in Malmesbury to pay for our Memorial in the Triangle, and it is safe to assume that a contribution would have come from Cowbridge. The design was by a young architect nephew of his. From a perspective point of view its siting is perfect. Equidistant from the buildings on three sides, its height is exactly half that distance. There was a large turnout of people to see the consecration of the memorial on Sunday March 20th 1921.

The Ordnance Survey Maps of 1900 and 1921 (the year Baldo died) show a great number of changes, many due to his influence. The billiard room has gained itself a rather quirky fireplace, the chimneybreast has a window directly above the fire, a typical Victorian conversation piece. The fireplace also boasts a few Art Nouveau tiles showing the influence of Charles Rennie Mackintosh. The strongroom too is an addition from that time, perhaps not in the best position, having three outside walls!

The billiard room c 1910

The estate has now gained a reservoir on high ground to the west and many more trees have been planted both in the park and near the main road. Rather oddly according to these maps Swindon, which must have grown considerably during these Railway Years, is one mile further away! In the boundary wall on the Swindon Road a letter box has appeared, suggesting that the family who live here are people of standing. This box disappeared again in the 1970s! Perhaps most importantly, the mill now supplies electricity, not only to the house but also the stables.

Cowbridge Farm built by Baldo must have been State of the Art; a Model Farm in fact. All of the outbuildings are red brick with upper story stucco covered in a mock Tudor style.

The billiard room 2005

A detail of the carving in the billiard room, thought possibly to be the work of Baldomero

Looking upstream from the mill house, note the boathouse on the left. The footpath to town is to the right of the river, now the roadway to Cowbridge Farm

Cowbridge Farm being built c 1910

Note the thatched roof on the dairy

Was the dairy always resplendent with pot plants?

The dairy originally had a thatched roof and porch. This sadly caught fire in the 1970s; when the fire brigade arrived the farmer had already coupled up the standpipe and the fire hoses which were attached to the dairy. Unfortunately the water supply was from the reservoir behind Cowbridge Crescent, which had very little pressure and so was of little help. The roof was lost and is now tiled but the building still retains much of its charm. The farm had a prize-winning herd of Dexter cattle, many of which were named after Baldo's female relatives, for example Cowbridge Ida and Cowbridge Ienne bearing names of two of his great-nieces!

One of the prize winning Dexter cattle with its calf, its name unknown

There was also a herd of Berkshire pigs, which are now considered to be a rare breed; in fact there were only 400 Berkshires on the 1990 United Kingdom census. With its placid temperament and distinctive markings of white feet, tail switch and white mark on its snout it is an attractive animal. The farmyard was complete with a selection of chickens and various ducks.

The mock Tudor cart shed c 1910

The same view 2005

These are definitely ladies from the "Big House" wearing felt wide brimmed hats and three quarter length duster jackets. Could they be great-nieces?

The Pattison family coat of arms; Baldo's English mother

Baldomero also extended the hallway of the house, fitting bigger windows and the staircase we see today, this is again almost certainly the work of Baldomero's young nephew. Standing on the stairs you can see many stained glass windows depicting various related family coats of arms, from both the English and the Spanish side of the family.

The main door c 1910 prior to its alterations. The building on the left, the clock tower was taken down in the 1980s. Strangely the magnolia growing on the other side had a preservation order on it and survived!

One window shows five horseshoes, the arms of Tobias Crisp, who died in 1643 who was Rector of Brinkworth and one of the English ancestors of Baldo's mother, whose family also have their crest here, as do the Bertodanos. Two cauldrons show that the family were "Ricos Hombres" i.e. rich men who raised their own troops in Spain to fight the Moors. The family's presence at the Battles of Navas de Talosa, the Hastings of Spanish history, and Rio Salado, are commemorated heraldically.

Baldo's great-niece Mary, a lady now in her 94th year, remembers spending her fourth birthday at Cowbridge. Her mother had told her that she was not to mention to anyone that it was her birthday, because it would look as if she was asking for presents. Mary was having none of that! She found Baldomero in his study and toddled up to him. The conversation went something as follows:

Mary, "Uncle Baldo, it's my birthday."

Baldo, (perhaps a little deaf) "What, what's that?"

Mary, "Uncle Baldo it's my BIRTHDAY."

The same view in 2005 note the magnolia tree: check its size in the 1870s
Photograph from Charles Kemble's album

Baldo did the decent thing and produced half a crown, Mary returned to the nursery and knowing that she had disobeyed her Mother hid the coin. Mary's elder sister Ida knowing what had happened "sneaked" to their mother. Judgment descended and Mary was sent to bed for the rest of the day. Luckily for the child Baldo's sisters heard the tale and pleaded successfully for her to be allowed back downstairs to celebrate her birthday properly.

Mrs Hetty Wicks, at the time of going to press 2005, a very hale 91 year old, has fond memories of the Bertodano family particularly the four sisters Henrietta, Alice, Louisa, and Mary.

At this time the family at Cowbridge employed as a cook Hetty's elder sister Carrie, and the four spinster sisters were very interested to hear of the forthcoming birth in Carrie's family. Soon after this Carrie was asked to take the new baby to the house for the sisters to fuss over and admire. These visits continued over a number of years. The two elder sisters became Godparents to Hetty, who was named Mary Henrietta after them; her own family shortened this to Hetty, the name to which she still answers to today.

Mrs Wicks describes vividly the approach to the house. This was through woodland alongside the Swindon road that is now Cowbridge Crescent - a small housing estate. Iron railings led her between the trees past a pet's cemetery, long since

29

gone, and a summerhouse, which still survives today. Sadly the long flight of stone steps and beautifully kept lawns and gardens she recollects did not survive. All that remains of the pet's cemetery is one headstone inscribed simply *Bobby*, this is to be found set into a concrete fishing platform by the Mill pond.

Louisa de Bertodano

Hetty remembers being given a velvet dress by the sisters and tearing it on barbed wire shortly afterwards, she has not forgotten the scolding she then received from her parents. She talks too of dances held on the lawns at the Big House, with bands playing and oil lamps in the trees lighting up the night. When the Bertodano family moved after Baldo's death, back to their London home in Regents Park, Hetty was still taken to visit them; she remembers them wearing long dresses and mop caps. There are other old ladies locally with similar stories of the generosity of the four spinster sisters towards them as children.

The stone steps leading down from the woods with Bertodano family members

Cycles were sometimes used for croquet at Cowbridge

Cycling was a new and very popular sport with young ladies; it was considered very daring for some to be actually sitting astride their cycles

The Italianate Gardens

Baldo died in 1921 and was buried at Kensal Green Cemetery in London. The house was put up for sale and the catalogue advertised amongst its assets the proximity to "the ancient market town of Malmesbury, and the stately monastic ruins of its famous old Abbey, and within about a mile of the mansion are post and telegraph offices, also the Abbey Church, Roman Catholic Chapel, and other chapels of various denominations, also good shops."

The kitchen gardens had peaches, nectarines and apricots, greengages plus vineries, melons, mushrooms and cucumber houses as well as all the normal vegetables. In the grounds was a miniature ivy-clad water tower with icehouse below it. Most importantly a generator, installed in the water mill, supplied electric power to the house and stables. A report appeared in the Wilts and Gloucester Standard in 1921 stating that Baldo's nephew had caught a twenty-one pound pike, thus confirming the "matchless fishing", which was advertised when Baldo bought the house.

A Noble Dining Room, Capital Wine cellars, twenty-seven bed and dressing rooms were also mentioned. A Dark Room for photography had been added above the outer offices. Many of the pictures in this book would have been first developed in that room. A recently constructed large and well-lighted workshop fitted with electric power for driving a lathe was also a Bertodano addition. It is ironic that within twenty years the whole mansion would become filled with engineering and electronics machinery and would later become the subject of a book "War Factory".

In 1922 Philip Hunloke bought the major part of the estate from Baldo's heirs for £25,000.

The millpond c 1910

The gardener with his own mixture of liquid manure in the drum behind him and a line of washing

The ladies pose for a photograph

The noble dining room

Drawing room

The terraces under a fall of snow

The King's Yachtsman

Philip Perceval Hunloke (1868-1947) was born with his twin sister Kathleen Sophy in London, where his mother "Happened to be at the time". As he had on occasions remarked, he took the Hunloke name when he was 46 years old.

Their father, also Philip, was a keen and very accomplished yachtsman who had been elected a Member of the Royal Yacht Squadron in 1858 where he was affectionately known as "Old Phil". Most of Philip Perceval Junior's childhood was spent at Cowes on the Isle of Wight, where he would have been surrounded by yachts and the associated trades, sail makers, rope makers and boat builders. He and other local children were invited to Queen Victoria's Osborne House to the children's Christmas party.

The family history states that Sir John Perceval first Baronet of Burton possibly went sailing with Charles II, known as the Father of Yachting, in the 1600s and that his son also John, second Earl of Egmont became First Lord of the Admiralty. Thus it was almost inevitable that "Young Phil" should follow the family passion for sailing and for yacht racing in particular.

Another ancestor, Spenser Perceval born 1762 became Prime Minister in 1809 but was shot in the House of Commons lobby by an assassin in May 1812. According to King's Sailing Master by David Duke; Perceval is buried in the Egmont family vault in Charlton church not five miles from Cowbridge. Anyone seeking him there will, however, be disappointed for his last resting place is in fact much nearer to Parliament at Charlton in London; a monument to Spenser Perceval can be seen in Westminster Abbey.

When he reached eighteen years old Philip appeared before the board to join The Blues, the Royal Horse Guards, but subsequently decided that an army career was not for him! Instead he returned to Cowes and to his first love - sailing.

Soon after his marriage in 1892 the Island Sailing Club elected Philip Perceval as Commodore and forty-three years later the same man, now Sir Philip Hunloke, was re-elected to the same post.

The Prince of Wales, the future King Edward VII, had commissioned a Scot G. L. Watson to build a royal yacht, Britannia, and it raced for the first time in 1893, though "Young Phil" was not onboard on this occasion, he sailed at the helm of the King's Yacht for a quarter of a century.

In 1904 Philip's Aunt Adelaide died and he inherited Wingerworth Hall in Derbyshire with a considerable estate of over 5000 acres. The Hall was a grand building of which little remains today. It was then that Philip Perceval became Philip Hunloke. Chatsworth House the home of the Duke of Devonshire is nearby and at that time held carriage rights to drive through Wingerworth to their castle at Bolsover. A house party from Chatsworth, which included the King and Queen, visited the new owner of Wingerworth in 1907; a man who could trace his ancestry back though eighteen generations to the first King Edward thus entertained the former Prince of Wales, now King Edward VII.

At the Olympic Games held in London in 1908 Philip Hunloke won a silver medal in the sailing class.

On the death of King Edward in 1910 the new King George V made Hunloke Sailing Master to his Majesty. From that date until Britannia's end only on one occasion did the yacht go to sea without "Young Phil" at the wheel: on that occasion he had to attend a funeral.

Major Philip Hunloke

During the 1914/18 war Hunloke joined the Royal Bucks Hussars but was made a King's Messenger and in this capacity he moved between Buckingham Palace, various Courts and the head quarters of our allies in Europe. In 1918 he returned to Wingerworth as a Member of the Royal Victoria Order, an honour bestowed upon him by King George V. He was also a Chevalier of the Legion d'Honeur, a Member of the Order of St Stanilaus (Poland) and a Member of the Redeemer (Greece).

The staircase at Cowbridge

Photo. Dick Grainger

Wingerworth was put up for sale in 1920, large properties were not selling however and although the land was sold, the Hall itself did not find a buyer and was demolished - with only a wing remaining today. In 1922 Sir Philip bought Cowbridge.

Local stories have it that the staircase at Cowbridge was brought here from Wingerworth. But this is untrue. The Cowbridge staircase we see today was fitted when the Bertodano family extended the hallway in the early 1900s. Robersons of Knightsbridge offered the Wingerworth staircase, plus the library and drawing rooms for sale, but the purchaser is unknown.

Hunloke continued to sail and in 1923 the Britannia took part in twenty-six races, winning eleven 1st prizes and twelve 2nd prizes. When racing she had twenty men onboard - but this sport was changing; the golden years of sailing were coming to an end. Rules were changed and even the yachts were changed. During the 1930s the years of Depression affected everyone. When George V died in 1936 it was known to be his wish that Britannia should be broken up.

King George V at the wheel of Britannia. Sir Phillip to the right
Photo. Central Press Photos

Some of the yacht's fittings were auctioned off and raised the sum of £1050.00 for King George V's Fund for Sailors. Her mast can be seen at Dartmouth Naval College and her boom has come home to the Isle of Wight as a flagpole at Carisbroke Castle. Under cover of darkness she was towed to a point South of the Needles, and sunk. Aboard a destroyer accompanying her were members of her crew including Sir Philip Hunloke the King's Sailing Master, who observed, "It was grim".

Sir Philip owned a sailing boat the Vera Mary and local stories suggest that it was a gift from the King. This is not thought to be true by the Hunloke family.

Sir Philip's passion for sailing was equalled only by his wife's passion for hunting and for all things equine. It was in fact his wife and eldest daughter who first viewed Cowbridge House as a potential future home. A major influence in their liking for the estate was the fact that the stables had electric light! Also in its favour was the proximity of the Beaufort Hunt at Badminton, and the Vale of White Horse at Cirencester. In was possible without too much travelling to hunt six days of the week. June Badeni (nee Wilson) remembers riding with the Beaufort at Cowbridge as a young child. When filling in her Hunt diary she decided that Sir Philip Hunloke took up too much space on the page, so abbreviated him to Sir P.H. so the former Young Phil had gained another title.

Vera Mary

When Major Hunloke moved to Wiltshire he brought with him to Cowbridge some of his staff, including Simkins the groom, who lived with his wife and two daughters in one of the estate cottages on the Swindon Road. "Simmy" as he was known became a well known character locally, always wearing riding breeches, highly polished leather gaiters and boots and with a handkerchief hanging from his jacket pocket. He has been described as "Quite a Dandy". He was often to be found in the

Public Bar at the Kings Arms in town. Whenever a stranger arrived he would find Mr Simkins at the bar billiards, usually looking very disgruntled. "Simmy" in fact had the ability to put the ball on a string through the billiards without knocking one down; this was accompanied with an expression of total disgust at his lack of prowess. The object of this now out of favour bar game is to knock over as many skittles as possible. If the stranger should fall for his ploy and accept the challenge of a game, the dandy's true skill was quickly revealed. Many visitors to Malmesbury discovered there were more ways than one to be "Taken for a ride" by Philip Hunloke's groom. His treatment to de-flea dogs was original to say the least. He was adamant that at midnight all the fleas on the left hand side of your dog would move to the right hand side to be replaced by those from the left. So all that was needed to rid the dog of fleas was to sprinkle flea powder on its spine.

Lady Hunloke at Cowbridge
Photo. Photopress. Johnsons Court. Fleet Street

Also arriving at Cowbridge with the new owners were Tom Stevens who had at one time worked on the Duke of Devonshire's estate at Chatsworth. His teenage son, also Tom, had the unenviable job of sleeping in the House quite alone, until the rest of the entourage arrived. This must have taken considerable courage in what is a quite large rambling house surrounded by trees. One night there was an awful crash that shook the rafters and must have almost petrified the young man. On inspection it was nothing more frightening than a pile of builder's piping which had collapsed in one of the rooms.

Young Tom met his bride to be when she took a job as parlour maid at Cowbridge and on their marriage they lived in Cowbridge Cottage, Lea, next door neighbours to his father and mother. A delivery man's nightmare, two Tom Stevens living next door to each other at two Cowbridge Cottages! It was there that his son and daughter were born, both of whom worked at the house after it had changed hands again. These cottages are just 200 yards from Cowbridge Cottages in Malmesbury where Simmy the groom lived.

Simmy Simkins Sir Phillip's groom. Shirley Hudson is the horsewoman
Photo. Shirley Hudson

In the early 1930s Tom left the Hunloke employment and trained as an electrician only to return to the Cowbridge estate soon after to carry on working in his new trade. In fact his cottage was enjoying the delights of electricity, whilst all the rest on the main road were still burning oil lamps. Tom managed this by running a cable from the generating plant at the mill, and connecting it to his cottage. The fact that there is the river Avon, the main Swindon Malmesbury Road, and at that time the railway line to be crossed he did not see as a problem! A slight draw back to the newly installed electricity was the fact that Tom could now be summoned from his cottage by an electric bell. The people at the Big House used a prearranged code to define their needs. Later in the story of Cowbridge, Tom became one of the best-loved characters in town under another uniform, whilst working for E. K. Cole.

Tom Stevens and workmate take a rest in the gardens. It is safe to assume that the owner is not in residence as this fountain is overlooked from every window in the front of the house!

Photo. Val Stevens

Between the pairs of cottages on the Swindon Road were the Cowbridge kennels - just far enough away from the house for the noise of the hounds not to be a nuisance. It was there that Major Hunloke kept his pack of Beagles who were a familiar sight around the area, further into the Cotswolds and even as far as Salisbury Plain. The former kennels is now the Willis Brothers Fencing Contractor's business. Following some building work an animal's gravestone was found inscribed "Gypsy a Great Sportswoman"; whether she was a beagle or a pet is not known.

Among the earliest tenants of Cowbridge Farm were the Bryant family. Their daughter Joan today a very sprightly 91 year old was seven years old when they arrived in 1922 and she left to get married in 1943 at the age of twenty one.

Revisiting the site almost seventy years later Joan remembers the outbuildings as "The new sheds". The dairy produced cream and butter for the Big House and she recalls picking large violets from the pathway to the dairy, to take to her schoolteacher. Alongside that path is a stone wall dividing the farm from Cowbridge House, she was not however allowed to pick fruit from the trees, even on the farm side of the wall.

Climbing the stairs of her former home she remembered a parrot, which spent some time with her family. The bird was so noisy that the only way to quieten it was to put it in the cupboard under the stairs.

The Dexter cattle had gone with the Bertodano family; at Cowbridge Farm the Bryants had only seven cows. The Hunlokes were more interested in hunting and sailing than farming, though Joan recalls that Lady Hunloke insisted on white turkeys, believing that their meat was whiter. Due to that whim the farmer's family had an incubator in the back bedroom hoping to raise more stock.

For Joan Bryant the long journey to school was up through the woods above the house, and she describes the spinney as having lots of flowering bushes, plus crocuses and daffodils. In winter, this journey was very different on returning home after a Saturday evening in Malmesbury. In the evening the shops would stay open until nine o'clock; Joan's father would play billiards with Simmy the groom at the Bear in the High Street, then after a final pint at the Black Horse, goodbyes were said at the top of Cowbridge Hill and the Bryants would set off though the trees and overhanging bushes. This often resulted in the frightened seven year old usually at the back crying out "I can't see", resulting in her father switching on his cigarette lighter, but any laughter was immediately shushed with "We don't want everyone to know we have been out".

The powerful sound of the water rushing though the sluice gates at the mill also made her nervous, but she has fonder memories of riding on the Malmesbury Bunk, as the train was called. As a small child she remembers it stopping in Lea fields opposite the farm and being lifted down to return home across the weir.

The local hospital held its annual fete at Cowbridge House in 1933; this was advertised in the Wilts and Gloucestershire Standard. The day almost proved fatal for one young boy.

At the fete a travelling show, which involved two lion cubs were allowed to perform. A two-year-old boy Patrick Fry from Burton Hill managed to crawl into the tent where the cubs were kept between shows. He was badly mauled by one of the cubs but was rescued by his mother and taken to the hospital in Burton Hill but did survive the attack.

He was much more fortunate than Hanna Twynnoy. One of Malmesbury's best-known characters she was a serving wench from the long gone White Lion hostelry in Gloucester Street. She died when a circus came to town and a tiger escaped and killed the young woman. Her gravestone found on the left approaching the Abbey porch tells the story in stone. Inscribed on it is "In Memory of Hanna Twynnoy who died on October 23 1703.

In bloom of life
  She's snatched from hence
  She had not time to make defence
  For tyger fierce
  Took life away
  And here she lies
  In a bed of clay
  Until the Resurrection Day"
The Wilts and Gloucestershire Standard tells the complete story.

Patrick Fry survived his ordeal and when an adult, for a while worked in the factory that was to become Ekco during the war years.

MALMESBURY.
Support Your Hospital
by attending the
FETE
in the lovely Grounds of
COWBRIDGE HOUSE
On THURSDAY, JULY 20th, 1933.

Many Attractions, including :
BABY SHOW, - DOG RACING, - CLAY
PIGEON SHOOTING, - FOLK DANCING,
CHILDREN'S CARNIVAL, Numerous SIDE
SHOWS, BOWLING, FANCY & NEEDLE-
WORK STALLS.
TEAS AND OTHER REFRESHMENTS.
DANCING—Music by Rialto Band.
Admission to field, 6d.   2.30 to 11.

July 15th 1933

Wilts & Glos Standard

MALMESBURY HOSPITAL FETE.

Business and Fun at Cowbridge House.

An energetic committee was entrusted with the arrangements of the annual fete organised in aid of the Malmesbury and District Hospital, which was held on Thursday in the delightful grounds of Cowbridge House, kindly lent for the occasion by Sir Philip and Lady Hunloke. The sun shone forth in full glory the whole of the day, the heat being tempered by a beautiful breeze which made the day an ideal one for an open-air fixture.

Last year the fete was held in Charlton Park, and an innovation was made by the provision of a programme of motor cycle races, but this year dog racing was substituted. Stalls and other inducements to visitors to part with their money were much in evidence, and there were very few who escaped the challenge by the enthusiastic ladies-in-charge to patronise their particular stall.

The carnival was marshalled in the Cross Hayes, and proved an interesting and valuable prelude to the fete proper.

The aim each year of the promoters is to exceed the total of the previous year and this has been achieved, the result of the 1930 fete being £217 15s. 10d., in 1931 £241 18s. 11d., and in 1932 £302 5s. 4d. Whether Thursday's fete surpassed that amount it is impossible as yet to state, though many of the large number of helpers were optimistic on the point.

A baby show, clay pigeon shooting, and dancing for a shield by schoolchildren in the Malmesbury Union area were amongst the many items in a full programme.

THE CARNIVAL.

The many characters represented in the Carnival, were the following: John Bull, Drummer Dyes, Beach Lady, Red Riding Hood, Market Gardener, Ye Olde Willow, Flanders Poppy, The Boy with the Nose, Economic Conference, O.K. Sauce, Newspaper Insurance, Kind Deeds, Departed Spirits, Drummer Boy, Pierrot, Irish Lassie, Jester, Snow (Bunny), Folly, Brigand Chief, Tramp, Bumble Bee, Indian Chief, Royal Mail, Flit, Strawberry, Hard Times, Golden Shred, Bunch of Violets, Two Baker's Boys.

THE STALLHOLDERS.

The following were the stallholders. Alderton has not got a stall, but sent gifts of provisions:

Brinkworth—Ices, Miss Livingstone; clay pigeon shooting, Captain Turner.

Brokenborough—Proceeds of rummage sale, Miss M. Clark.

Corston—Sweets, Mrs. A. W. Chubb; wheelbarrow competition, Sir John and Lady Pollen.

Crudwell—Bowling, Colonel W. B. C. Burdon.

Charlton—Bowling, Rev. F. Hudson; darts, and weighing machine, Mr. A. Greenfield.

Easton Grey—Rummage stall, Mrs. Guy Gibbs.

Foxley and Norton—Tea buffet, Mrs. Tom Rich.

Hullavington—Provisions, Mrs. O. T. Harry.

Hankerton—Hoop-la, Rev. A. Packer.

Lea and Cleverton—Cakes, Mrs. Kingston.

Luckington—White elephant stall, Miss B. Spence.

Milbourne—Bran tub and doll, Mrs. E. Whitting.

Minety—Cocoanuts, Miss Ludlow-Hewitt; supper, Miss Kirby.

MALMESBURY HOSPITAL FETE.

CHILD MAULED BY YOUNG LION.

A report of this successful gathering was given last week. The weather held up beautifully fine throughout the day.

Quite a panic was caused during the evening by a shout that "the lions are loose." An itinerant show had been admitted and occasional exhibitions of two young lions were given. During the intervals the animals were allowed exercise in the marquee in which they were shown, but during these intervals no person was allowed inside. In some way, however—it is conjectured by crawling underneath the canvas of the tent—a little boy, Patrick, the 2-year-old son of Mr. Harry Fry, of Burtonhill, Malmesbury, managed to get inside the marquee, where it was quickly mauled by a lion, said to be ten months old. The child was so badly clawed about the neck and face that Dr. Battersby found it necessary to insert nineteen stitches in the little sufferer at the hospital, whither he was conveyed under the care of Sister Killeen, who chanced to be on the field.

It is stated that the mother heard the child scream, and that as she rushed into the marquee to rescue her child, the other lion, which was also loose, approached towards her. The poor woman's agony is better imagined than described, and the little child is also suffering from severe shock. Mrs. Fry says that as she got into the tent one lion was standing over her child.

The little one, at the time of writing, is progressing favourably.

The Hospital Management Committee desire to express their grateful thanks to all who helped at the Hospital Fete by service, by gifts, by loans, or by transport, or by any other means. The fete was very successful, and the Committee hope soon to publish a financial report. The Committee are very grateful to Lady Hunloke for coming from London to present the Carnival prizes, and for helping in many other ways; to the Countess of Suffolk for distributing the baby show awards; to Master John Battersby (son of Dr. and Mrs. F. J. G. Battersby) for selling lavender; to Elizabeth and Rosamund Lawrence, who sold buttonholes; and to the Evening World for their Melody Van. Mrs. E. Ramsay, who as hon. secretary worked untiringly for the success of the fete, was assisted at the teas by Mrs. M. H. Chubb and Mrs. R. M. Moore. Mrs. T. Rich's assistants at the buffet included Mrs. W. T. Drew, Mrs. W. B. Carter, Miss Few, Mrs. Hurst, Mrs. Gough, Miss G. Nice, and Miss N. Bailey.

Corston won the folk danting Schools' Shield, and, having won it three years following, now retain the trophy.

July 22nd 1923 Wilts & Glos Standard   *July 29th 1933 Wilts & Glos Standard*

Sir Philip offered the house for sale and moved to Hampshire in 1939.

MALMESBURY - WILTS

THE
COWBRIDGE ESTATE

For Sale by Auction in Lots
On the 28th day of June, 1939
At 2.30 o'clock.

Solicitors :
Messrs. BIRD & BIRD,
5, Gray's Inn Square, London, W.C.1.

Agents and Auctioneers :

Messrs. ALFRED SAVILL & SONS,
51a, Lincoln's Inn Fields,
London, W.C.2.

Messrs. JOHN D. WOOD & CO.,
23, Berkeley Square,
London, W.1.

Sale catalogue

The EKCO factory

When Sir Philip put the estate up for sale and moved to Beaulieu in 1939, no one could have foreseen the dramatic changes ahead for Cowbridge House. It was never again to be a family home and the gardens would in time disappear. Some of the staff were kept on but with very different duties. Simmy the Dandy groom became a pig man and The House would become a War Factory.

In August 1939 at Southend on the Essex coast a meeting took place involving the management team of a radio and electronics factory which would change Malmesbury forever. Eric Cole had originally sold electric bells and radio batteries. He then heard about a freelance journalist, William Verrells, who complained that it should be possible to connect radios to the main electricity supply. The two men got together and their first radio set was made in an old cigar box and connected to a light socket! These early radio sets were sold locally and all profits ploughed back into the new business. By the late 1930s, Cole's firm was Southend's biggest employer next to tourism, giving work to over three thousand people. Eric Cole and his Southend workers had just begun to produce the latest technological craze - television sets. The trade name EKCO derived from the initials of the manager Eric Kirkham Cole, highly appropriate for a business involved in radio and Radar sound waves!

Cole and his team were very much aware of the problems developing in Germany, and the near inevitability of war. It was obvious that Southend would be an easy target for Luftwaffe bombers. Because of this danger the factory was closed down and various departments dispersed to sites around the country. For this reason Maurice Lipman, who at that time was running the Electrical Appliance division at Southend, was sent on a mission.

Lipman's brief was to find a building that could be used as factory premises within 100 miles of London to the west. The premises had to be near enough to a town to recruit workers. Lipman was not told what would be produced, only that it would be of television size and that eventually the factory would employ about 200 people. After a weeklong search he met up with Eric Cole and others at the Bell Hotel in Malmesbury, to report on his progress. By this time war was imminent and Lipman was informed that the search was even more urgent and that total secrecy was needed as to future operations.

William Winch, a local doctor had moved to Malmesbury in 1938 from Southend where he had been a Public Health Inspector. Dr Winch knew Eric Cole well as they had sailed together and played golf. In 1935 they had spent a motoring holiday in Germany with two others. It was probable that Cole was more than interested to see the radiolocation pylons in place on German airfields.

What is certain is that Doctor Winch mentioned the availability of Cowbridge House to his friend Eric Cole, who in turn told Lipman to look at the property.

The House met most of the requirements; it had its own mill to generate electricity. It was surrounded by trees which gave it some cover, and it had 14 acres of grounds which gave room for expansion. Also included in the sale price of £6,500.00 were six cottages. On behalf of Ekco Mr Lipman bought the house, the grounds and some of the cottages the day before war was declared.

Ekco temporarily closed down their Southend factory and moved into properties at Aylesbury in Buckinghamshire, taking over a hat factory and a printing works. They also moved to factories in Woking, Surrey and Rutherglen on the Clyde near Glasgow. Their Head Office was at one of the Rothschild mansions near Aylesbury. But Cowbridge was the very first of the country properties to be used by Ekco when they moved away from the threatened environment of Southend.

Throughout the war years Radar played a very important role and it has been suggested that the outcome of the war would have been very different without it. In the late '30s, Radar was still in its infancy. The German air ship Graf Zeppelin had carried out a reconnaissance flight over the south and east coast of England to discover what wavelength was being used by our listening stations.

It was here in Malmesbury that so much research and development on Radar took place. Experienced workers were brought from Southend to work and, more importantly, to train the new staff who would soon be employed.

Taking down walls in order to enlarge rooms altered Cowbridge House internally. The stables and other outbuildings were changed into workshops and stores; machinery was brought onto the site, most of it from the parent factory at Southend. One of the rooms was converted into a canteen.

The Stables

At the break up of the estate, Cowbridge Farm had been sold to a local farmer, who for a number of years supplied the factory with milk for the canteen. The herd of cows still came through the grounds of the Big House in order to reach fields on the far side of the Swindon Road, and this practice continued throughout the war years and well into the 1960s. The gardener was kept on and for years supplied the workers with fresh vegetables and fruit including grapes and peaches from the greenhouses in the large walled garden. The garden also supplied boxes of fruit for the Ekco factory at Southend. Bob Greenaway recalls bringing bread and rolls to Cowbridge House daily from Gay's Bakery at the nearby village of Lea. He was not too pleased when the canteen was moved from the ground floor to upstairs as the bags of flour, which he also delivered, weighed 140 lbs!

The Stablehand's accommodation

Maurice Lipman as Works Manager accused the local town of being very feudal and described the Town Council as being something out of a Charles Dickens story. The local solicitor reminded him of Gilbert and Sullivan's Pooh Bah! Despite this he did manage to rent premises in the town at 43/45 High Street. Staff working on V.H.F. Fighter Control System, which was later used in the Battle of Britain, used the very large building behind it. These workshops were known originally as Special Products Division, where experimental work was carried out. This was later named the Western Development Unit. The building which is now Gable House Surgery, was used as a storeroom, remembered by one of its workers only because it was so very cold!

Knowing that the workforce would soon increase dramatically, Lipman also rented houses for use as hostels for the workers. The Priory, which burned down in October 1967, was situated on what is now the Swindon Road roundabout. There was Halcombe House on the Foxley Road and Rodbourne House (now the Cleeve). Here Mr Lipman lived in one of the wings with his wife who ran the hostel as her War Work. When the Navy started to use A.S.V. (Air to Surface Vessel) Radar, ratings were drafted to the hostel to be taught installation and maintenance. Their ration books and mess allowance were passed onto Mrs Lipman and for a while the hostel became known as H.M.S. Rodbourne.

With the increase in personnel, more workshops were needed; the courtyard was roofed over, and one large glasshouse was demolished and replaced by a capstan lathe shop. One former employee recalls that he worked for a number of years in what was an aeroplane packing case stood on a concrete base by the riverside! An assembly plant was built on the front lawn where, in the days of previous owners, croquet had been played and dances had been held.

Wartime extension

This meant destroying the grand terrace and the steps that had so impressed the young Hettie Weeks during her visits to the Bertodano sisters at the turn of the century.

Extra output meant a heavier demand for water, which took pressure away from some of the nearby houses. This resulted in a very irate telephone call to the factory manager from a lady who claimed this had interfered with her bathing routine. The suggestion was made that she changed her bath time, reminding her that "There is a war on". The only reply was a slammed down telephone soon followed by a letter from Ernest Bevin the then Minister of Labour. The letter told Mr Lipman that he had very much exceeded his authority. He chose to ignore it!

With the very real danger of bomb damage the factory formed its own fire-fighting brigade. A three-inch water main ran around the factory buildings and included the farm. Red painted wooden cabinets were placed around the estate and held hoses, nozzles, standpipes and the keys to open the necessary valves. There was also a petrol-driven fire pump, which has recently been traced.

For a period during the summer of 1940 Eric Cole's wife and children stayed in Malmesbury at Tower House, the home of Cole's friend Dr Winch, in order to escape the dangers of bombing at Southend.

Ekco Fire Service Helmets

Due to the worsening situation in Europe, France had surrendered and the British Expeditionary Forces had been evacuated from Dunkirk in 1940. A great number had been wounded, many had returned home without their weapons and all the heavy artillery was left on the battlefields of France.

Desperate measures were required. Young men who had failed the medical exams to join the Services plus "Old Soldiers" from the First World War who were past call up age were enlisted into a new group. The L.D.V., Land Defence Volunteers came into being. Quickly christened Look, Duck and Vanish they were soon renamed the Home Guard, but known to everyone as Dad's Army. Ekco staff had a large platoon which included those who had not been allowed to enlist because of the importance of their work.

It seemed almost certain that the Germans would invade Britain and defensive measures were taken. The Military decided to build "Stop Lines"; these were designed to slow down invading tanks by using and increasing natural obstacles already in place. Rivers, canals, railway embankments and escarpments had artificial obstacles added to them - such as very deep ditches which would serve as tank traps and concrete bollards.

Stop line Green, which was built to protect Bristol from a land invasion runs for over 100 miles from south of Weston-super-Mare through Wells, Radstock, Wellow, Bradford on Avon, Chippenham, Malmesbury, Avening and Stroud. Then onto Framilode north of Gloucester and on to the River Severn.

A selection of fire fighting equipment as fitted around the factory buildings

Ekco's own Home Guard platoon

Also incorporated into this defensive line were over 150 reinforced concrete bunkers or "pill boxes". These were to be manned by men armed only with rifles and machine guns. Their job was to repel tanks! Many of the pillboxes were at main roads and bridges and if the invasion took place some of these bridges were to be blown up in an attempt to slow the enemy's advance. One such bridge was at Cowbridge.

There are in fact five concrete bunkers within a mile of Cowbridge House; the nearest in a small copse near Willis Bro's Fencing Company alongside the river at Cowbridge. A second slightly smaller of a different design is in the hedgerow behind Kemble Close; another is only two fields away behind the houses at Knoll House. Pillbox four now stands guard over a private tennis court at Cowbridge Lodge on the opposite side of the road and the fifth is roughly half a mile downstream where the river Avon and the disused railway almost meet. A few of the remaining concrete bollards can still be found on the riverside just downstream from the house, others have been used to form part of the weir. It is also possible to see railway sleepers driven into the banks of the river where it is particularly shallow. The sleepers were intended to stop tanks from crossing and some remain at the sewerage farm outfall at Cowbridge.

Pill box situated behind Cowbridge Crescent

Although built with extreme urgency in the summer of 1940 the defence lines were never tested. Work stopped during the autumn because 'The Few' had won the Battle of Britain. The fight for supremacy of the air was over, thanks in no small part to Radar. Cowbridge House had played its own part in that fight.

In 1940 Ekco started to recruit more unskilled female labour. Some of these women left jobs in cookery and other forms of domestic service or as stable hands working for the gentry. This form of recruitment did much to alienate the factory from the town. Phyllis Elms (nee Pike) well remembers joining the factory and staying until her daughter was born in 1946. Like so many of the young women, she met her future husband at work. George came daily with his workmates from Chippenham, in a covered wagon, not quite the Prairie Schooner it sounds, more a flat bed lorry with a canvas cover over it. The senior workers always sat in the centre, because though the canvas kept the rain off, anyone touching it got very wet indeed. This 'privilege' was reserved for junior workers.

At this time women were enlisted either to join the forces, the Land Army or to work in factories. Phyllis is still in contact with friends from the West Country drafted into Ekco at that time. Her memories are tinged with sadness, for many of these girls married men who did not return from the war. After a while her dexterity was noticed and she was taught coil winding. This often earned Phyllis bonuses. She visited a destroyer in Bristol docks on one occasion and on another was introduced to John Cunningham, one of the best-known pilots of World War Two.

"Cats Eyes" as Cunningham was known visited the factory both to see the latest developments on the Radar front, but also to provide a morale boost for the staff. He was at that time the equivalent to today's class "A" celebrity. Cunningham was the first man to shoot down an enemy aircraft using Radar. Only one of his 20 "kills" was in fact achieved in daylight. It was Air Ministry propaganda that provided his nickname early in the war. The Ministry alleged he had exceptional night vision due to an unusually high consumption of carrots. This was in an attempt to take attention away from the newly invented Radar. "Cats Eyes" was every schoolboy's hero, despite being responsible for the boys being told by their parents to "Eat up your carrots so that you will be able to see in the dark". Wing Commander Cunningham remained a household name in aviation well into the 1950s when he often starred at the Farnborough Air Shows.

There were other "bonuses" to working at Ekco. Phyllis explains that George was a skilled sheet metal worker, and very inventive. He made his new bride a set of fish knifes from sheet metal and smuggled them out of the works!

He also made a poker with a very ornate head. This came though security hanging round George's neck, a very early Medallion Man. Even more original was a picnic basket to fit the rear of the car they had bought. This too was of sheet metal and smuggled out by the man responsible for toilet cleaning and rubbish disposal. He in turn rendezvoused with a delivery driver at the rear of the factory, and the basket was at home when the pair arrived at the end of their shift. Still in use it now doubles as a blanket box. One worker needing electric cable at home, wound a considerable length around his body until he began to look like a Michelin tyre advertisement. He then borrowed his rather large friend's overcoat and walked out of the gate undetected. He was doing fine until he attempted to mount his bicycle. The weight of cable upset his point of balance and he fell and knocked himself out. First Aid staff were called and all was revealed! It was well known that anything "won" from the workshop could be taken into the woods alongside the house and thrown over the fence to be collected at the end of your shift. A strange honour amongst thieves did not allow you to collect anything other than your own piece. With just about every conceivable engineering and electrical skill available in the various workshops there was very little that could not be made to your own specifications! Given a little time there was a man who could get you just about any make of second hand car!

One male Line Manager could supply the young women with underwear when that was not easy to come by! Oliver Pike remembers dashing up St Mary Street in his lunch hour to John Motts the local bookmaker's with his workmates' bets.

"Cats Eyes" Cunningham

Another slightly less conventional skill available was that of a "Faith Healer" Mrs Curd from Brinkworth. Terry Thomas tells of his father who suffered from a painful shoulder for many years and consulted the lady. She laid her hands on the affected shoulder saying that she would send her blue spirit. The shoulder was cured. When some women were photographed with Mrs Curd, there was a face in the background looking like a Chinese Mandarin. She claimed it was one of her friendly spirits! This story was passed onto me with a smile but no photographic proof.

Jean Boulton from Little Somerford had started work in the Council Offices at 10 High Street, which she enjoyed, but her mood changed when she found she was conscripted to work for a Mr Stevens in the Production Office at Ekco. She described him as a "Not very nice man, with red hair and a temper to match". Jean's biggest problem was the fact that she knew no engineering jargon, and simply could not understand Mr Stevens' cockney accent. She admits that her office job was the result of "the old boy network", but she was unhappy enough to ask personnel for a transfer to the assembly line! The news must have got back to her boss, for the next day there was a letter on her desk from him. Inside was a five pound note and a written apology "Sorry I could not get you chocolates", rationing was making them impossible to come by. Jean Boulton says he must have felt guilty for £5.00 was a lot of money then, as much as she earned a week in fact. Pre war men working on the local farms were getting around £2.00 per week. Jean's hours were long, 8am till 8pm, with a 5pm finish on Tuesdays. She also worked Saturday mornings. For a large part of the year the workers would arrive and leave the factory in the dark.

Jean Boulton

As well as being well paid Jean was well fed. She remembers Simmy, Sir Philip's former groom, and "his" pigs. These were converted into ham and bacon which helped feed the staff at a time when rationing was making life difficult for everyone. Many factories were encouraged to keep pigs if it was feasible. The pigs were fed any kitchen scraps; the agreement being that when the pigs were slaughtered half of the produce went to the factory and half to the Ministry of Food. Simmy had two very different herds one looking very well fed and one looking very scraggy! The second group's destination was definitely not the factory kitchen they were destined to go the Ministry of Food!

Jean used to cycle to work and to the dances held at the factory. She remembers Harry Gold and his Pieces of Eight appearing there on more than one occasion. She was returning from one of the dances around midnight on the night when an aeroplane dropped a stick of bombs behind the council houses at Lea Top. Her boyfriend pushed her into the ditch to avoid the blast. Jean thinks the bombs were meant for an anti-aircraft crew based at Coach House Farm near the Little Somerford turning. A local story has it that this crew hit the bomber and that it crashed near Reading.

Office staff 1943
Back row L to R: Alec Emery, Phylis Saye (nee Hislop), Jennifer Fry, A.N. Other and
Mr Bull wearing his Home Guard uniform
Front row, L to R: Leslie Tudor (errand boy), Myrtle Lewis, Iris Winton, Grace
Coleridge, Mrs Pengelly and Florrie Law (nee Wood)

It was at Little Somerford Hill that Jean and an old gent Joey Upperton had another narrow escape from serious injury. She was in her own words "Going like hell down the hill" on her bicycle on a very dark night. Batteries were almost impossible to get during the war years so she had no lights, and saw the old gent much too late to avoid a collision. Her front wheel disappeared between his legs at some force and they both fell over. "Now you've done it" the old man gasped and as a recovery measure took both himself and Jean into the nearby public house for a brandy!

One of Jean's duties was the weekly update of a production chart in Mr Lipman's office at the top of the staircase. Jean found him to be a short stocky, pleasant man with a very attractive younger wife. She was asked on one occasion to sit in on a meeting in the boardroom and take shorthand notes. This made her very nervous knowing that Mr

Lipman would be taking the Chair with high-ranking Army, Navy and Royal Air Force officers also present. To put herself at ease she wore her best dress, sent to her by some rich friends in America - black velvet with lace trimmings. She stressed that people did get dressed up to work in offices then! When she arrived at work, dolled up to the nines, she was greeted with "You look like that advert". When she asked which one she was told "The one with the woman all in black, 'Keep Death off the road'". "This put me down a bit" said Jean "but I did the shorthand O.K."

Staying on the fashion front Jean recalls a Mr James who was in charge of the Paint Shop. He was very popular with the young women for if they had a blue dress but black shoes, and asked him nicely, Mr James would spray the shoes blue in a very short time. He did have a rather limited palette, but would colour coordinate shoes whenever possible.

Many of the early employees speak of one particular fireplace in the old House. This had been brought to Malmesbury by the Hunloke family from their home in Derbyshire and was made from Blue John. This material is unique to a now exhausted mine from that area and very much sought after. There is now no trace of that particular fireplace and to date I have been unable to trace its whereabouts!

Jim Haggerty who worked in the Model Shop, and his wife Anna from Personnel, tell of a fellow worker collecting the fruit of the horse chestnut tree, to take home for his children to play "conkers". Because of a recent spate of thieving he was stopped at the Gate by Security and asked what was in his bulging bag. His answer "conkers" justifiably annoyed the guard who invited him to empty his bag. This was done with obvious glee by the worker, who then walked home. It is not recorded if he was stopped the next evening!

One particular security guard was more unpopular than most, a very tall heavily built man who could not walk without a swagger. At the same time each evening he would lock the gates, leave his hut and with a tray under his arm march to the canteen to collect his supper. He would soon return holding the tray in front of him, still giving the impression of officiousness. One evening someone removed a manhole cover in his path. He lost some of his swagger as he disappeared from sight - but he managed to save his supper.

In 1942 Ekco was allocated 12 pre-fabricated bungalows paid for by the Ministry of Aircraft Production. These were to be erected on a field owned by Ekco just above and to the west of the house. Whilst taking measurements in the paddock, (now Cowbridge Crescent) Lipman and his colleague were challenged by the lady who owned the field, who was exercising her two ponies. She wanted to know what they were doing. They duly explained the situation, saying she would soon receive a requisition notice and reminding her that there was a war on. This prompted the question "Where will my daughter put her ponies?" She was answered with a courtly bow and the reply "Madam that is not for me to say".

In the very early war years there were suggestions that Cowbridge House had been taken over by a group of rich men for their sons to live in and avoid call up into the services. Because of the highly secretive nature of the work the factory was unable to refute this. It was probably at around this time that the factory's extra offices at 43 High Street, Western Development Unit or W.D.U. was renamed by the townsfolk as the War Dodgers Union.

The well tended gardens at the pre-fabs pictured in the 1960s

Originally the pre-fabs were for Ekco workers only. But after the war more pre-fabs were added to the original 12 and several were given over to the local council for townspeople. This, too, caused problems as Ekco still had the right to allow their workers to move into any of the pre-fabs that became available; the townspeople saw this as queue jumping.

Pre-fabs were intended as temporary housing. Most people lived in them for over 30 years and talk of them with great affection.

The pre-fabs were of very modern design with good sized rooms; the kitchens had built-in units including a wash boiler, pantry, broom cupboard, cooker and a fridge - long before most people could boast of such luxuries! The coal fire in the living room had air ducts, which heated the bedrooms, and the bathroom had a hot rail to warm the towels! Each garden had a coal shed plus another general purpose shed. Generally speaking the whole design was well ahead of its time.

The locals knew the area as Tin Town, though the exterior walls were made from asbestos and the framework from aluminium which was plentiful at the end of the war, as the country no longer needed aeroplanes in vast numbers. There was however a huge housing shortage. Thousands of bungalows were made and erected all over Britain. Colin Gabitas who brought up his family at Cowbridge Crescent remembers being told by one old soldier that he was shown pictures of pre-fabs whilst serving in Italy! Our Servicemen were introduced to the bungalows as the "The Homes for Heroes" that would be waiting for them on their return to Blighty.

From the very opening of the works, the firm was aware of its vulnerability from air attack; the many trees on site helped to conceal its true identity, but as a further safety measure any stores or lorries outside the factory for any length of time were covered over with camouflage netting.

Houses replaced the bungalows in the mid '70s. It is just possible to see Cowbridge House between the trees

In 1942 the factory had its narrowest escape. Derek Stratton, then a young boy out with his brother, remembers seeing a German aeroplane drop flares near their home at Crab Mill in Lea. Their property was joined to its neighbour Southfield Farm by a causeway over swampy ground into which the first flare fell and was soon extinguished. However the following flares set a hedge alight close to the river and the railway. Had the first flare burned longer, it is believed by the Stratton brothers that the German crew would probably have mistaken the two farms with their many outbuildings, for Cowbridge, the target they were obviously trying to find! It is alleged that Lord Haw Haw broadcast the fact that the Luftwaffe knew the whereabouts of the factory and that they would "Pay it a visit". There are reports also of bombs falling near the Ekco hostel at the Cleeve at Rodbourne. Hetty Wicks remembers reports of a hit behind the council houses at Lea Crescent, not very far from the factory. This is confirmed by Jean Bolton's story of cycling home on that particular night and finishing up in the ditch!

Many local people remember the lunchtime concerts, and Workers' Playtime a popular variety show from the radio era. This started in the very early 1940s as a morale booster initially with a six week run. It was the first radio show to go "on the road" and proved to be so successful that it continued until 1964; from The Blitz to The Beatles in fact. Ernest Bevan the Minister of Labour often appeared wherever the show was taking place to tell the workers what an important part they were playing in the War Effort. When the programme was announced on the radio the venue was never disclosed; it was always "From a works canteen somewhere in Britain". Many of the top stars of that time did their stint on the show, Harry Secombe, Ted Ray, Petula Clarke and Jimmy Edwards were regulars. Ekco worker Terry Thomas (not to be confused with the comedian from that era) remembers seeing a very smart red sports car arrive at the works for a concert in the early '60s driven by Jon Pertwee, later to become well known as "Doctor Who".

On one occasion a very pretty young woman in W.A.A.F. uniform arrived at the factory offering to give a concert. This she duly did which was greatly appreciated. What was not so welcome was the visit a few days later by an Air Ministry security man. He explained that the young woman was "One of ours". She had not been asked to show a pass at the gate and had been successful in "planting" imaginary bombs in various parts of the factory. Security was a priority after this visit.

Vera Punter worked at Ekco during these war years and was responsible for Drawings, which were kept in the "The Library"; this had been the billiard room when the Bertodano family lived here. The strong room held the most secret of the drawings. Long after the war Vera realised the significance of her often being asked by her boss "Do you ever get letters from abroad?" Anyone corresponding with people from "abroad" during these very uncertain times would have come under very close observation.

Much later on, that same strong room held the firm's supply of precious metals as did the butler's pantry, both being very secure.

During the early war years the Drawing Office was situated in what had been the conservatory. Cynthia Dickens (nee Drake) worked there as a tracer from 1948 until 1957. This job entailed tracing a pencilled drawing done by a draughtsman of any new component, onto specially prepared pure Irish linen, which was opaque and very strong. Prints were then taken from these tracings and passed onto to the various workshops needing them. Almost all of the sheets used at Ekco were pre-stamped TOP SECRET, though some came on unstamped rolls. Cynthia describes the pens they used as being like the sharp beak of a bird with a screw to adjust the size of the beak opening. This determined the thickness of the line. The pens were fed Indian ink through a dropper bottle. Electrically powered print machines later replaced the older printers, which had previously used ammonia and are now museum pieces.

The young women soon found alternative uses for the Irish linen; washed several times it made superb underwear, pillowcases and even cot sheets. This was a time of rationing and an example of the ingenuity of the young women.

Working in the old conservatory had its drawbacks, the roof leaked and could ruin any drawing. One woman continued working under an umbrella, whilst most just covered their work with thick cardboard sheets and waited for the rain to stop. At one stage the tracing office was partitioned off from the other offices with an asbestos screen, which meant a considerable detour to reach any other department. On returning from lunch one day the women discovered that someone had sawn a doorway through the asbestos. This certainly shortened further journeys but did not meet with the boss's approval.

Cynthia Dickens recalls taking part in a one-day strike by the drawing office staff in the early '50s for better conditions and pay. After picketing the works entrance for a couple of hours they spent the rest of the morning in Malmesbury, had lunch then went home. In fact Cynthia, unmarried at that time and still living at home did not go home until her usual finishing time. Her parents never knew about their daughter's day on strike!

Queen Mary

When Cynthia did marry she bought plastic buckets and bowls from a shop situated at the security gate. These items were manufactured by Ekco at Southend, but made available to all employees; she still has them in use almost fifty years on.

Without doubt the most prestigious visitor during the early years was Queen Mary, who spent most of the war years at Badminton Park nearby. Queen Mary had known the house from the time when Sir Phillip Hunloke had been the King's yachtsman. She was given a guided tour of the factory but there is no record of her comments regarding the condition of the house she had once known.

As the war years ground on the morale of the workers slumped. Many of the women had been conscripted from far and wide. They did not want to be in Malmesbury and they were not wanted here by the townspeople. Every shortage of food and supplies was magnified by the fact that the town's population had more than doubled. The cinema was often full of "unwelcome visitors". Any cosmetics that arrived in the local shops were snapped up by the young women from the Ekco. It was not unusual to find no fish in the fish and chip shop. All of these things and more, were blamed on the factory. Many of the workers were living as lodgers in local houses. This made life difficult for the owner who had another mouth to feed at a time of great shortage. Despite bringing extra money to the town, the "men in suits" were not welcome. They gave an appearance of wealth but a local bank employee is on record as saying, "They may look down on us, but there is more money under the beds of some of the local families than they will ever have."

Things really came to a head when the owner of the Old Bell put up a notice in his hotel, "Employees of E.K. Cole are not welcome in this Bar". Within a very short time he was asked politely if he would remove it by the Chairman of E.K. Cole in Southend. This he did.

It was at about this time that Mass Observation was asked by Mr Lipman if they would come into the factory. He hoped to learn something from their report to help lift morale and boost output. Mass Observation was a much-respected social research organisation mainly concerned with recording the huge social changes during the war years.

Propaganda films and posters showed women rushing eagerly to the service of their country however Mass Observation told a very different story.

An observer would be drafted into a given situation incognito. Their job was to observe and report on the workers, the conditions, the hours of work, attitudes of both staff and management and anything they thought relevant.

The author Celia Fremlin had first worked for Mass Observation just prior to the outbreak of war. She then distinguished herself reporting on the London Blitz whilst working "under cover" at a Lyons Corner House as a "Nippy" as the waitresses were known. Soon after she found herself working "In a small factory in Wiltshire as an unskilled hand in a machine shop". This was of course Ekco at Cowbridge. Only four people knew of her true identity and the purpose for her being at the factory. She worked the same hours and lodged at Rodbourne House with other workers. Celia Fremlin was well aware that if the other women knew her real reasons for being there all spontaneity would be lost and any reports would be useless. Her method of taking notes was interesting. "I needed to make my recordings as inconspicuous as possible, but the method I found most useful of all was to establish a reputation as an almost obsessional letter writer. Using a writing pad perched on my knee during tea breaks and slack periods, I would start the page with "Dear Emma" or "Dear Sammy" or whatever, and proceed to record dialogue as continuous prose, without capitals, punctuation or quotation marks, which renders it almost unintelligible to the casual glance".

Neither the factory, nor indeed the town, is named in the original book published as "War Factory" in 1943, though both are easily recognised by anyone who knows them well. Malmesbury and Ekco are however mentioned in the introduction to the 1987 reprint.

Reading between the lines of the first paragraph gives some indication of the upheaval about to be suffered by both the factory and the townspeople. "In a tiny country town of ancient cottages and winding streets, with traditions going back to Saxon times, there has suddenly sprung up in a matter of months, a modern war factory employing nearly 1.000 people staffed mainly by brisk town-bred men who have no connection with the locality".

Her first impressions graphically describe Cowbridge as it was in those early war years, "The actual site of the factory is what was two years ago a large country house, set in lovely grounds about half a mile outside the town. In spite of the sound of machinery and a mess of new buildings, some of the original charm remains, a lovely polished oak staircase leads up to the offices; old beams and latticed windows strike a pleasant incongruous note. Outside, a curving drive arched over with trees form the entrance, and just in front of the main building is a stretch of water surrounded by bushes and shrubs, and is still inhabited by a family of ducks".

The stone Gazebo

The wooden bridge both enjoyed by staff

In her reports everyone's name is scrambled after being sorted into income levels (or Class). Just slightly, non-politically correct!

"A"   Rich People
"B"   The Middle Classes
"C"   Artisans and skilled workers
"D"   Unskilled workers and the least economically or educationally trained third of our people.

When the new assembly shop was built on what had been the Italianate garden, Celia Fremlin was on hand to record one of the women workers voice her regrets, "I don't like this new place. We used to be upstairs it was nice like a real old mansion, you went up a lovely polished staircase there were oak walls and everything. I used to look forward to coming to work it was so pretty.

Assembly room c1940

"You could have all the windows open and look out on the lawn, there was a fountain and a goldfish pond where this place is built now. You could see the grass and the flowers in the sun and the fresh air came in the summer. It's all clammy down here and you never see the sun any more. Do you know I sometimes have to think is it morning or afternoon now? You don't know if it is summer or winter, day or night now. I don't like it!" This statement by an uneducated country girl is surely as poignant as anything penned by Oscar Wilde in Reading Gaol.

There is a footnote by the Works Manager about the workers complaints about the lack of sunlight. "The assembly hall was actually built to Ministry specification; no windows were allowed larger than 3 sq ft or below a level of 9 ft. Such windows as these are to be obscured by anti-shatter material, and while all this is in the interest of employees' safety, it is naturally galling to those who remember the previous surroundings. In a town this would not be noticed, but when it is known there are trees and fields outside, it is objectionable but unfortunately unavoidable."

Today the assembly shop again looks a depressing sight, a large empty space, concrete floor and brick walls with those high windows. Below ground on both sides are two corridors approximately sixty feet long, though to call them tunnels would be more descriptive. These 'tunnels' have quite small rooms off both sides looking like monastic cells. Built as Air Raid Shelters they were used as storage space in later years, but some workers did actually work down there.

L to R: Joyce Matthews, Alex Baker and Gladys Tidy at an assembly bench

Pauline Evans worked at the factory from 1941 until `46 starting in the Cable Shop; here she sat in front of a wooden board with a number of nails knocked into it. Various coloured wires were passed between the nails and joined together, then waxed string was wound around them to join and protect them and create a pre-formed loop. She and many others did this from 8am until 5pm having a set number to complete each hour. Pauline was fortunate as her grandmother lived in the Lower High Street, so each lunchtime she hurried there for a meal. It is said that the High Street was full of the workers cycles during Ekco's lunch break!

Gladys Tidy who was at the factory from the late '40s until 1972 also started work in the coil winding shop. She, with two other women, were caught looking at some photographs during her shift. She insists the photos were totally innocent, holiday snaps or something similar. The women were originally to be suspended for a period for this terrible crime! Their boss however relented, but as a punishment moved them to Assembly. Anyone reading War Factory will see this action does seem to follow a pattern, other workers were told they might be moved to this particular shop as a deterrent for behaviour that did not meet with approval!

Gladys however looks back fondly of her time at Ekco. She remembers that the young women would listen to Housewife's Choice and Workers' Playtime on the radio. They would place one old-penny bets on whichever popular song would be the first to be played, winner takes all!

If any worker left their workplace to go to the canteen before the hooter sounded, then the radio would be turned off as a punishment. This of course was the time of "clocking in"; every employee had their own card, which had to have a time stamp made by the clock, at the beginning and end of his or her shift. The firm gave everyone three minutes "grace" but if you clocked in at four minutes after the hour you should have started work, it cost the worker a quarter of an hour's pay. This was standard practice. Clocking in someone else, to save them losing money, could cost you your job!

The old wooden sheds put up in the early '40s for Radar research still stand on site, though there is now no sign of the tall stone tower built in the woods. This was originally the water tower that had supplied water to the house and the fountains when the gardens were in their prime and an icehouse had also been in use below the tower. The tower had been heightened in the early '40s, to be used for testing the new Radar sets. This was done by quite simply carrying the assembled set to the tower, then through a door and up a great number of steps for the test to take place. Jim and Anna Haggerty remember one new employee being sent to carry out this task. Somehow he missed the doorway, but spotted a ladder, which was a fire escape (a straight iron ladder attached to the outside of the tower). He managed to complete the climb still carrying the completed installation. Imagine the shock he gave the engineers when his face appeared amongst the trees at a window over 30 feet high. Later on a lift was fitted to the tower and Ivor Chambers well remembers the day that he somehow managed to overload it. Several very expensive and vital Radar sets came crashing down to ground level. Ivor was convinced that his career was finished as far as E.K. Cole was concerned, but he was told that the engineers could now test to see how the sets would respond to an aircraft crash. He still thinks he was lucky to continue in employment. He is one of the few people who remember Mr Lipman the first Works Manager; it is Ivor's proud boast that as an office boy he filled the boss's ink well!

Radar sheds 2004

Radar sheds 1960

It is believed that the Malmesbury Bunk, the railway that ran from Dauntsey to town, was used early on as one of the first moving objects "found" on Radar.

A Works Sports and Social Club was started up by Ekco, with Government backing, in the hope that the workers would integrate with the locals. This was not a great success. Most of the workforce was not here in Malmesbury by choice. They saw the situation simply as an interruption to their normal life, and wanted only to return to the life they knew. The original clubhouse was in Ingram Street, the flats that are now Cartmell Close. One of the problems highlighted by Celia Fremlin in "War Factory" was the fact the club was organised and frequented by the factory authorities. The staff felt that it was not for them, "Too posh for us" and "It is more for the Office girls" were typical statements. Jean Boulton, who worked in an office, enjoyed the social club and remembers going there to hear classical music on records with another worker, who lodged at Rosemead House in Culver Gardens.

The cinema, now St Michael's Close, was more popular and the social club started a showing on Sunday evenings. This was primarily for the staff, H.M. Forces were allowed in next. Finally, provided any seats were left, and as a rather poor relation or an afterthought, the townspeople were offered a seat.

Ekco and the very latest thing television woo Malmesbury townsfolk at the Town Hall

After the war Ekco continued to manufacture for the Ministry of Defence but many workers were made redundant and others given the opportunity to transfer to the parent factory at Southend. The Cowbridge factory took on work for other organisations including the Atomic Energy Establishment at Aldermaston. They were also involved with Blue Streak Space programme.

In the 1960s tape recorders, radios and radio gramophones were made at Cowbridge and in 1962 the first car radio, which could be removed and carried in the hand, came off the factory line. The "tranny" or transistor radio was born!

Thermotube heaters - who is the pin-up pop star?

The factory manufactured many electrical appliances, including Thermotube heaters. These were used in the horticultural trade and were simply metal tube room heaters some as long as sixteen feet. Economy 7 room heaters produced in 1963 were used in the home. These proved to be popular for a while and the factory ran a night shift for the first time since the war years. They were very bulky objects, which had inside them large concrete blocks that were heated by electricity at night when the cost was cheaper; the theory being that the heat was released during the day when it was needed.

In 1963 the factory was further extended and Ekco was absorbed into the Pye group of companies. Not long after this the Telephone Manufacturing Company "TMC" joined forces to form PYE/TMC, which was involved with both developing and producing telephone equipment on the site.

Switchgear being made at Ekco

Green Shield stamps were used as an incentive at one time in the 1970s. Any employee who recruited a new worker was given 18000 stamps. One such "winner" is pictured with Personnel Manager John Hislop.

As the years went by so the site became much more of a factory and major building took place in the mid 1970s and again in 1982. By this time the factory had now become A T & T and Phillips Telecommunications UK Ltd.

Though the house still stood, no trace of the gardens remained. Busses no longer brought the workforce as everyone now came by car. Most people parked either between the river and the Cowbridge Farm drive or on the car park which had been built where once had been the kitchen gardens and the many greenhouses. A bridge was built over the river to allow another car park to be made amongst the trees alongside the old Malmesbury Bunk Line, the long disused railway line.

The kitchen pictured in the 1960s, note the potato peeler at the back and the chip machine in the foreground. One potato at a time! This kitchen supplied three separate dining rooms

The staff canteen from the same era

Works Social and Sports Club

The building that started as the Works Social and Sports Club in the early war years later became the Ekco Sports and Social Club. This club moved from its original home in Ingram Street onto the factory site, using the old mill house as its clubroom. Many workers and townsfolk remember the club and its many activities with great affection. Well into the 1970s the club entered and often won the Best Decorated Float at the local Carnival. It also had its own Miss Ekco, who always entered the Malmesbury Carnival Queen competition. There were also very successful Hockey, Cricket and Football teams. Our picture shows the 1949/50 Football team with the EKCO logo on their shirts. At that time the home fixtures were played in a field behind the Silk Mills owned by Mr Edmunds of Cowbridge Farm. He also owned the adjacent dairy where the players' wives and girl friends boiled up water for the players to bathe

Carnival float
Back Row, L to R: Zebra Pitman, Dick Grainger, Dave Chappell, Glyn Farmer, Vic Vincent, Tom Stevens, Vera Hoffman,
Front Row: Mrs Osbourne; June Cambourne and Miss Bourne
Photo. Val Stevens

at the completion of the match. The Annual Football Dinner menu in 1950 boasted Tomato Soup, Cold Chicken Salad and Fruit and Ice Cream it finished with Cream Cheese and Biscuits, which says everything about those austere times. Food rationing was still very much in evidence.

Football team photo
Back Row, L to R: Ron Clark, Bev Thompson, Norman Scott, Norman Clark, Ted Smith (Capt.), Brian Goulding and John Stratton
Front Row, L to R: Leighton Chapple, Fred Shepherd, Don Lacey, Norman Knapp, and Tony Twine

Photo. Norman Clark

Fishing was one of the most popular activities from the outset. This is hardly surprising with the proximity of the Avon and remembering the 'matchless fishing' as advertised in the Cowbridge House sales catalogue from the 1800s. Terry Thomas who has completed over 40 years as Secretary of the fishing club was mentioned in the Cowbridge Gazette of 1964. He had caught a 13oz dace, which beat the then record held by the Bristol Avon Club.

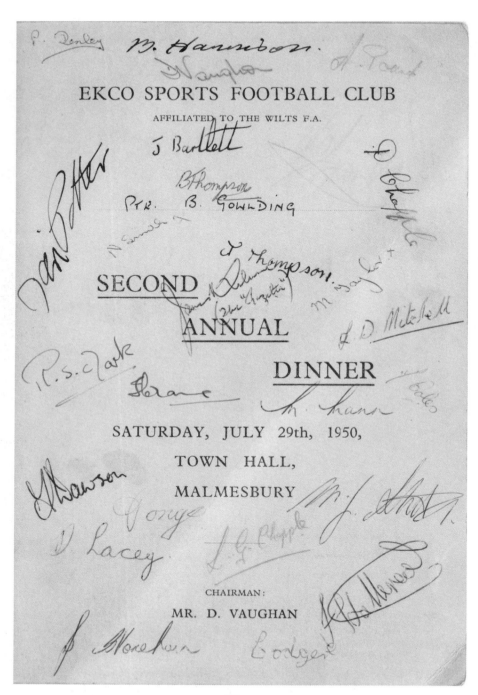

Menu

Norman Clark

Cricket Team c 1950
Back Row: Gill Pierce, Jim Haggerty, John Legg, A.N. Other, Jim Aylward,
Ted Dorling, Dave Chappell
Front Row: Richard Curtis, Len Fox, Norman Godwin, Bill Kimber, A.N. Other
Photo. Dick Grainger

Fish collected after the toxic leak

Photo. Terry Thomas

It was a disaster for the fishing when a worker in the plating shop inadvertently opened the wrong valve and discharged toxic poisons into the river. Fish were killed for miles downstream and it took a long time to repair the damage done to both the river and the reputation of the fishing club.

Terry Thomas who had started work at Ekco in the early 1960s is pictured at a horizontal milling machine

The Social Club produced newsletters under various headings over the years. These allowed all members to keep abreast of developments in the branches of the social club, as well as providing a "shop window" for the staff. The 1983 edition of the TMC/EKCO advertised a walking day in the Wye Valley for members and also advertised a four bedroomed semi detached house in Crudwell for sale at just under £49,000.00.

Terry Thomas shown with one of the finials, (much repaired) from Cowbridge House roof. These are made from copper and are lightening conductors

Cowbridge House, Malmesbury.

Several of the lightening conductors, shaped to look like stone finials, can be seen on the roof in this postcard of the house

Ron Peel collection

EKCO SOCIAL AND SPORTS CLUB

THE COWBRIDGE GAZETTE

President - Mr. S.A. Clodd.   Vice President - Mr. C.B. Cleland.

Chairman - Mr. L. Cooley.

SEPTEMBER, 1964.

We are pleased to know that Mr. Clodd and Mr. Cleland have again accepted the positions of President and Vice President of the Club, and both have sent their very good wishes for the coming year.

The new Committee, with officers as elected at their first meeting, is as follows:-

THE THRIFT CLUB is again in action for anyone wishing to save in this way towards a pay-out at Christmas.

CHRISTMAS PARTY. Note the date - 18th December - and watch for further details in due course.

THE ANGLING CLUB continues to be the most consistently keen and active group in the Club.

Congratulations - to Norman Fisher who has advanced from minnow snatching to catching a few grayling still in the learner stage; to Terry Thomas for his 7 lb. 2 oz pike which gave him many anxious moments and a mild heart attack; to Dick Granger, on catching a 2 lb. trout - his first big enough to take home for tea; to Gordon Chin and Dave Richardson for many hours patrolling Ekco A.C. waters as Bristol Avon Water Bailiffs; to the weed and tree clearance gang, namely Bob Parslow and Terry Thomas, assisted by Stan Woodman who not only drove them up the wall, but into the trees as well. Fish were hard to find, but not leaky waders. The work was hot, but feet were cool, as members quickly found out.

The most outstanding feat has been achieved by Terry Thomas, who beat the Bristol Avon River Board's record for a Dace. The previous record was 10 ozs. and Terry's weighed 13 ozs., thus winning him fame in the national press. Well done!

Cowbridge Gazette excerpts

Photos. Terry Thomas

In the early 1960s all the skittle teams were Men Only, but at one General Meeting held in St Mary's Hall Frances Axam and Gladys Tidy went along and asked if they could form a ladies team, this met with the men's approval and the first women's team appeared, calling themselves "The Roll Ons". The name taken from the revolutionary ladies undergarment from that time which did exactly what it said. Before its invention all women's corsetry was laced up. There is no record as to which was the more uncomfortable to wear, but it is generally agreed that women had great difficulty getting the Roll Ons on and men had just as much trouble getting them off! When one of the members of "The Roll Ons" was married at the Abbey her team-mates were there to "support" her - complete with skittles.

The "Roll Ons" Left to Right: Hillary Talbot, Gilly Webb, Glenys Webb, Janet Russell, Glad Tidy, Frances Axam, Lydia Webb, Margaret Punter, Joyce Thornbury and Pauline Hicks

Photo. Gladys Tidy

Outings to various theatres were commonplace as were the dances and the occasional 'Tramps Ball' when everyone dined on fish and chips. They are still talked about.

Many silver haired gentlemen - plus some with now very little hair at all - will tell you smilingly that, "Ekco dances were where you went to find the girls". The majority of the workforce was young women and many married couples first met at these dances.

All of these functions were held to raise funds for the Annual Christmas Children's party.

Gladys Tidy fondly recalls one particular Christmas Eve when she visited the Black Horse with her husband Howard and other workmates during the midday break.

Everyone enjoyed a lunch where food was secondary to the liquid on offer! She says that "No one was drunk but we were all quite merry". One friend serenaded everyone with "When father painted the parlour" whilst standing on a table. They went back to work down Cowbridge Hill quite happily, and probably noisily, only to be "shushed" as they approached the security gates by the more sensible members of the group. They managed to pass the Gate without too many giggles only to have the duty guard call out "I want a word with you Mr Tidy". At this, the women, including Mrs Tidy, ran off back to work leaving Howard to face the music. He was at this time a charge hand, so it was with some trepidation that he entered the security hut. Much to his relief he was told he had won a raffle prize and was given a tin of Craven A cigarettes.

A Tramps Ball

The Third Annual Sports held in 1945 at Gays Field Cowbridge invited competitors to compete at sack race, egg and spoon race, and slow bicycle races. There were also hurdles and high jumps, an ankle competition and the chance to take part in a 'wheelbarrow race'. This did not in fact involve wheelbarrows but instead there was one male and one female competitor. The young woman would either be wearing shorts or would tuck her skirt into her knickers. She then lay face down in front of her partner. He placed her ankles under his arms and held her just above her knees. When the race started she "ran" with her hands - thus becoming the 'wheelbarrow'.

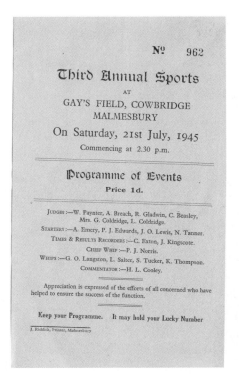

Nº 962

Third Annual Sports

AT

GAY'S FIELD, COWBRIDGE
MALMESBURY

On Saturday, 21st July, 1945

Commencing at 2.30 p.m.

Programme of Events

Price 1d.

JUDGES :—W. Paynter, A. Breach, R. Gladwin, C. Beasley,
Mrs. G. Coldridge, L. Coldridge.
STARTERS :—A. Emery, P. J. Edwards, J. O. Lewis, N. Tanner.
TIMES & RESULTS RECORDERS :—C. Exton, J. Kingscote.
CHIEF WHIP :—P. J. Norris.
WHIPS :—G. O. Langston, L. Salter, S. Tucker, K. Thompson.
COMMENTATOR :—H. L. Cooley.

Appreciation is expressed of the efforts of all concerned who have
helped to ensure the success of the function.

Keep your Programme.   It may hold your Lucky Number

J. Riddick, Printer, Malmesbury

- EVENTS -

TIME	
2.30	100 yards, Female
2.33	100 yards, Male
2.36	Potato Race, Female
2.40	100 yards, Female Championship
2.45	Slow Bicycle Race, Female
2.49	220 yards, Male
2.54	220 yards, Female
3.0	Slow Bicycle Race, Male
3.5	Veterans Race
3.10	100 yards, Male Championship
3.14	Four-legged Race, 2 Males and 1 Female
3.18	220 yards, Female Championship
3.23	440 yards, Male
3.28	Wheelbarrow Race, 1 Female and 1 Male
3.30	440 yards, Female
3.35	Ankle Competition
3.35	220 yards, Male Championship
3.40	High Jump, Open and Championship
3.45	440 yards, Female Championship
3.50	Sack Race, Male
4.00	**TEA**
4.30	440 yards, Male Championship
4.35	100 yards Hurdles, Females
4.38	100 yards Hurdles, Male
4.45	Egg and Spoon Race, Female
4.50	100 yards Hurdles, Male Championship
5.0	100 yards Hurdles, Female Championship
5.5	5 miles Race
5.7	Egg and Spoon Race, Male
5.10	440 yards Shuttle Relay—Departmental, Male (team 4)
5.20	High Jump, Female Championship and Open
5.25	Sack Race, Female
5.35	Flowerpot Race, Female
5.45	440 yards Shuttle Relay—Departmental, Female (team 4)
5.55	Tug-of-war, Male
	Tug-of-war, Female
6.30	Children's Races
7.00	Presentation of Prizes by Mrs. M. I. Lipman

*Sports day programme
Loaned by Gordon Williams*

*Sports day programme
Loaned by Gordon Williams*

Young women made the national newspapers and caused a few red faces in the early 1960s. This of course was the time of Women's Liberation, Free Love, the Profumo Trial and the Sexual Revolution. At one club dance a group of Exotic Dancers had been booked to perform. And they did! Nudity was unheard of on stage, but was seen in the canteen on this occasion! It has been said that not all the performances took place on stage. Malmesbury was not quite ready for this; men were invited to remove the stockings of some of the ladies - and more! It certainly made headlines in the *News of the World*. Malmesbury survived - but questions were asked of the person who had booked the group.

The highlight of the year for many people was the Christmas Parties - and the children's Christmas party is remembered by just about everyone who attended it. Somewhat oddly this event always took place early in January.

The children's party started in the 1950s when food rationing was still in force. Originally for children of the staff, the party soon grew to accommodate all the children in town. David Forward remembers with great affection waiting for the Party invitations to arrive. These were not sent to the parents of the children. Each individual child had his or her invitation brought to its door, by the postman. David describes the cards as being special, being coloured and having scalloped edges.

Where are they now? Children enjoying an Ekco Christmas party
Photo. W. J. Barratt Cirencester

Parents were issued with labels to attach to their offspring. They were told at what time the coach would collect the children, also the time they would be returned. On arrival the label was torn into three; one part stayed on the child; one went with his or her coat to a specific cloakroom and the third part was given to a coach steward. Everything went like a military operation. A coach took children up to the age of thirteen to the factory canteen, which was unrecognisable. The walls had been covered with Disney characters, all hand drawn and painted by Ken Gough from Hullavington who worked as an electrician at Cowbridge. Each figure was just the size of a child and can be seen in the background of our photo, which shows helpers at one of the parties - interesting to note that each young woman nurses both a child and a cigarette!

Decorations hung from the ceiling and there were balloons everywhere. The stage had been converted into a living room complete with fireplace and this too had been decorated for Christmas. The children were fed jellies and ice cream, and tinned fruit; a rare treat in those austere times. After this it was time for games followed by a film show of cartoons, something, again, which at that time was almost unknown to the vast majority of the children. This was long before every household had television and a trip to the local cinema was a special occasion. There were stage acts and clowns - all put on by the factory staff. The highlight was of course Father Christmas's arrival, heralded by a bell being rung very loudly in another room. All the children had been gathered together and were then told "Father Christmas has just come through Brinkworth". The children were then told to shout very loudly so that HE would know where to turn off the main road. They were then told it was not loud enough and he had passed on through to Sherston. After a few "diversions" like this, the noise generated was similar to a Beatles concert!

Note the cigarettes! Totally unacceptable today

Photo. Val Stevens

Imagine the excitement of 400 or so children as they eventually saw Father Christmas arrive. All eyes were on the stage to watch a sledge actually come through the fireplace.

Tom Stevens had arrived at Cowbridge as a very young man and had guarded the house prior to Sir Philip Hunloke's arrival with his family. Tom stayed on to work for EKCO and is remembered as Father Christmas by literally hundreds of Malmesbury people. Throughout the year he would pay visits to Swindon Market to buy presents, bring them home and wrap them ready for distribution at the Children's Party. His own two young children were totally unaware of his double identity so this he could only do after they had gone to bed!

During the party the stage and sledge were prepared and the window at the back of the living room had snow falling behind it! This was managed by simply putting a fan inside some shuttering behind the window then feeding the fan with small pieces of torn up white tissue paper.

Tom's daughter Val went to the party along with all her friends and used to go up and receive her present with them - blissfully unaware of her father's double life! As well as the huge white cotton wool beard and disguised voice, Tom always wore calfskin gauntlet gloves to help hide his identity. One Christmas he had mislaid the gloves and had to appear without them. When it was his daughter's turn to receive her present she sat on Father Christmas's lap, and looked down to discover she was looking at her own father's hands. All her dreams were shattered and she burst into tears, Father Christmas was not real!

Young dancers entertain at the party.
They are: Maureen Ockwell, Daphne Gott, Hazel White, Janice Carey, Pat Price,
Maureen Wicks, Val Stevens, Miss White, Pamela Carey
Photo. Val Stevens

A few years later Val with other girls actually took part in the stage shows for the younger children - our photo shows them looking like a Shirley Temple audition. All the mothers had decorated their daughter's dresses by sewing onto them the coloured tin foil wrappers off chocolates, saved throughout the year to represent jewels.

Derek Tilney helped raise funds during the latter days of the EKCO party by running a football sweepstake, which met with some opposition from various anti-gambling groups. Derek recalls that the committee always borrowed several mail sacks from the Post Office in which to stack presents ready for distribution. They were very much aware that as the line of children got shorter the child at the very end of the line would get more and more worried to see the pile of empty sacks getting bigger, and the supply of presents getting smaller. This was solved by almost filling several sacks with crushed newspaper, but with presents visible in the neck of the sack! Any new male volunteers who wondered if there were going to be enough presents to go round and enquired as to "What will happen if we run out?" were told "If you have a watch we will have that because little boys love watches". Derek says that the next time they saw the same volunteer he would be looking rather sheepish but not be wearing the watch quite so prominently. Uncle Mac from the B.B.C.'s Children's Hour was a V.I.P. guest at one of the parties.

S.T. Smith Works Manager, Jacky Grimes Mayor and Tom Stevens

Photo. Val Stevens

After 25 years as Father Christmas, the Town Mayor and the Works Manager, as a "thank you", presented Tom Stevens with a barometer. Just two years later in January this man who as a young lad had slept in the house alone as a caretaker for Sir Phillip, felt too unwell to don the red cape and beard for the Christmas party. To maintain the family tradition his son Charlie stepped into the breach, but in February Tom was dead. In some ways the end of an era.

Coaches leave from the factory

Photo. Dick Grainger

Harringay Arena, fourth from the left in the lower picture is Charlie Stevens alongside "Father Christmas" Tom

Photo. Dick Grainger

Harringay Arena programme

Another social function that is remembered by many employees is the Ekco Silver Jubilee in 1951. All the workers, plus husbands and wives were taken by coach to Harringay Arena in London to see Tom Arnold's Rose Marie on ice, starring the then Olympic skating champion Barbara Ann Scott. This invitation was extended to the other Ekco factories around the country. Many coaches left Malmesbury and everyone was given a packed lunch for the journey and a souvenir programme. It was at this occasion that Eric Cole was presented with a portrait of himself painted by Frank O. Salisbury C.V.O. Salisbury had studied at the Royal Academy and had painted King George V and King George VI and also Queen Mary as well as both Winston Churchill and Clement Atlee.

A Message from the Chairman

This is indeed a happy occasion for me, both personally and as Chairman of E. K. Cole Limited. It is not often that we can all gather together under one roof, and I would like to say how delighted I am that our Silver Jubilee presents such an opportunity. I hope that everyone present, including wives, husbands and friends, will have a thoroughly enjoyable evening.

Eric K. Cole

Reproduction of portrait by Frank O. Salisbury, C.V.O., to be presented to Mr. E. K. Cole by the Company's employees as a mark of esteem and appreciation.

Eric Cole portrait

The Ekco Works Children's Entertainment Committee was still going strong into the 1970s and was solely responsible for the Christmas Party.

EKCO WORKS CHILDREN'S PARTY – SATURDAY, 10th JANUARY, 1970.

Oranges - 280 at 8d each	£9. 6. 8d.
Squash - 4 x 1 gallons at 16/-d per gallon	£3. 4. 0d.
Sausage Meat - 6 lb. at 3/4d per lb.	£1. 0. 0d.
Puff Pastry - 6 lb. at 1/6d per lb.	9. 0d.
20 Loaves at 1/9d each	£1. 15. 0d.
1 x 48 Crisps	£1. 4. 0d.
8 lb. Bananas at 1/6d per lb.	12. 0d.
24 eggs at 4/-d per dozen	8. 0d.
1 x 12 Cress at 4½z per box	4. 6d.
5 lb. Cheese at 3/-d per lb.	15. 0d.
4 lb. Butter at 3/4d per lb.	13. 4d.
3 lb. Ham at 6/6d per lb.	19. 6d.
Plates, Doyleys and Serviettes	10. 0d.
300 Paper-bags	6. 0d.
300 Vending Cups	16. 6d.
Tea, Sugar, Milk for 60 Helpers	£1. 0. 0d.
280 Cardboard Plates at 2/9d for 10	£4. 1. 9d. 3. 17. 0
280 Ice Cream Cases	£4. 1. 9d.?
340 Bridge Rolls - 2/-d per dozen	£2. 17. 0d.
340 Cakes at 4½d each	£6. 7. 6d.
4 x 1 gallons Ice Cream - 16/-d per gallon	? £3. 12. 0d.
	? £43. 19. 6d.
+ 20%	£8. 16. 0d.
	£52. 15. 6d.
+ Staff Wages	£21. 2. 10d.
Total ...	£73. 18. 4d.

FRM

6th January, 1970

Compare today's prices with the 1970s

However in the changing society in which they found themselves it was decided in 1978 to discontinue the Christmas party. The family atmosphere was less apparent and people were becoming more self-reliant. The children were used to colour television so a film show would hold no charms for them. Sadly the Committee decided to disband. What should be done with the money still held by the club?

The staff were asked for suggestions and the most popular idea was to buy a bed for the local hospital. Funds were in fact available to purchase two beds. After some negotiations the Wiltshire Health Authority wrote to the Committee thanking them but adding that there was no longer a need for the beds!

After further consultation with staff, £50.00 was given to the Malmesbury Boxing Club and the remaining £241.67 to the youth club at the Cartmell Centre then based in Ingram Street. So the money ended up in the same building as the original headquarters of the Works Sports and Social Club.

Cards from Cowbridge

There are a surprising number of different postcards showing pictures of Cowbridge House and its grounds. Some of the differences are not great and occasionally the picture shown on two or more cards is exactly the same, but the printing is in a slightly different position or a different typeface has been used. Such cards are sought after by serious card collectors but I have tried to avoid showing those that are to similar.

The first postcard was first sold in this country on October 1st 1870 after the Post Office Act of that year sanctioned their use. One side of the card had to be used for the address only, no message allowed. The message was to be written on the "picture" side of the card as can be seen from one of the examples shown. It was not until 1902 that the Post Office relented and at last agreed to allow the message to appear on the same side as the address. This of course allowed the whole of the face of the card to be used for the picture.

Famous diarist the Reverend Francis Kilvert was well to the fore with his postcards. An entry for Tuesday October 4th 1870 tells us "Today I sent my first postcards to my mother, Thersie, Emmie and Perch. They are capital things, simple, useful and handy. A happy invention."

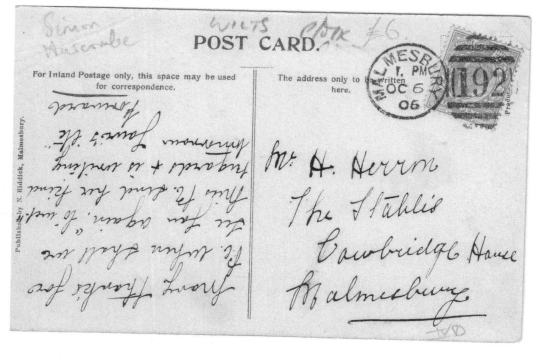

Kilvert was born at Hardenhuish near Chippenham and preached at Langley Burrell, not far from Cowbridge as the crow flies. He also preached at Clyro near Hay on Wye on the Welsh borders. Kilvert was a great visitor of houses large and small in both England and Wales. Sadly no record exists of him visiting Cowbridge.

At the turn of the century postcards were used in the same way that E-Mail, or the mobile phone are used today. In large towns as many as five postal deliveries took place in a single day and it was not unusual for a card to posted at noon to a local destination to inform the recipient that the sender would be home late that evening!

One of the postcards shown is addressed to The Stables at Cowbridge and has the message written upside down. This is quite common on old cards and is thought to be intended to stop unauthorised people i.e. the postman, reading the message. As with the majority of cards the message is of remarkably little interest to anyone other than the person for whom it was intended.

Many young women working in service used cards as a method of keeping in touch with their families and with other young women in the same job. With little education they would find letter writing a daunting prospect but a card would be well within their capabilities. A postcard had its own formula, the greeting was invariably followed by the sender commenting on their own health and enquiring after the health of the recipients. The weather often received a mention and this left just enough room to sign off.

The postcard from Edna to Mrs Biles at Buscot near Lechlade dated 1931 is possibly an example of a member of staff at Cowbridge writing to a previous workmate. Was Edna "poached" by the then owners? We will never know.

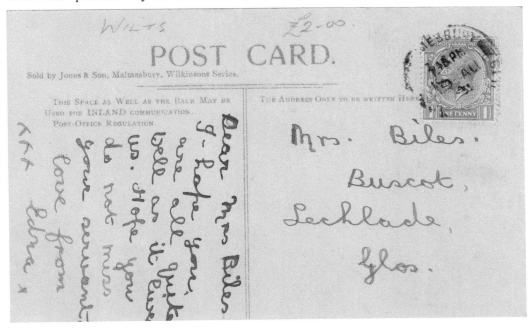

Many of the cards shown were almost certainly produced by the owners of Cowbridge House. Both the de Bertodano and Charles Kemble family photograph albums show pictures that are identical to some of the postcards in this collection. It is also known that Baldomero had built a dark room specifically for his photographic work.

J. Riddick of Malmesbury Avonvale Service J.B. & S.C., R.F. Houlston Chippenham, W.H.S. & S LDN and the "Famous Series" of Thompson and Barratt

Swindon, W.D.M. & Co Cirencester and Jones & Son Malmesbury are some of the many firms who printed postcards of Cowbridge House.

Thanks are due to the Malmesbury people who so willingly allowed me to copy from their collections of local postcards: John Denly, Sue Pratt, Simon Hurcombe, Gordon Williams and Ron Peel whose collection is surpassed only by his knowledge.

A Malmesbury Lace Worker.

PHOTOGRAPH BY W. DENNIS MOSS.

OOXII

POST CARD.
THE "CECILY" SERIES.

£25

Write Here for Inland Postage only. | The Address only to be Written
| Here.

This to Ruth White, wife of
Joe White who used to work for
Mrs Kemble at Cowbridge.

W. D. M. & CO., CIRENCESTER.

Cowbridge House.

Cowbridge House

Cowbridge House, Malmesbury.

Potterne 19. sept.

Wednesday if I can get away. I'm writing to N.J. will tell them where you have been to

The Rose Garden. Cowbridge House. Malmesbury.

Cowbridge House (South). Malmesbury.

COWBRIDGE HOUSE, MALMESBURY.

Tomkins & Barrett Swindon.

Cowbridge House, Malmesbury.

Cowbridge House, Malmesbury.

Cowbridge House, Malmesbury.

Cowbridge, Malmesbury.

Cowbridge House, Malmesbury.

W. Hanks, Malmesbury.

Cowbridge House, Malmesbury

The Drive, Cowbridge House. Malmesbury.

Cowbridge House (S.E.). Malmesbury.

The Lake and House. Cowbridge. Malmesbury.

The " Terrace's " Cowbridge House, Malmesbury.

What Now?

As you drive past the site of its former glory today, Cowbridge looks very different. The Malmesbury Swindon road now carries a lot of traffic, both pairs of cottages look much as they always have done, some of the copper beech trees have survived as has a splendid cedar of Lebanon and a Sequoia. These two trees near the main road are all that remains of the plant life from the Italianate Garden. Dominating the view today are two modern three storey office blocks and the security building.

If you walk along the drive to Cowbridge Farm you soon pass the Mill Pond which looks as tranquil as ever, though the mill house is still there but it has no mill stream. That was filled in during building works in the 1980s. From that viewpoint it is possible to see the main door that features in so many of our photos. At the rear of the house there still survives a very old wisteria scrambling over the building, flowering well in late May despite having no attention. Standing in solitary splendour is a Magnolia Grandiflora shown in one of Charles Kemble's photographs as a young sapling in 1875, which flowers well in early June. There is a large car park today on what was the walled kitchen garden. It is still possible to identify a part of the old walls. In the woods stands Baldomero's petrol store pagoda; nearby is the sad sight of an almost derelict stone summer house. Surrounding the stone summer house but almost entirely hidden under ivy is all that remains of the balustrading that made the gardens so striking.

The second and third floor windows on the front of the House are still intact and look as attractive as they appear on the many postcards of the House. The conservatory went during the latter War years. At this same time the two storey brick extension which housed the assembly room and canteen were built over the lawns and gardens; this we can still see today.

Internally the staircase, built in a mock Georgian style is easily the most attractive feature and is still impressive. Spacious and flooded with light through its many large windows it does not take a lot of imagination to picture guests being greeted there in the past. Today plastic buckets are on the stairs to catch leaks from the roof!

The rest of the House shows the ravages of time; there are few signs of the wood panelling that would have been such a feature in the main rooms. The open courtyard was covered over in the early war years. The billiard room does still retain some carving, but overall we find the House in a sorry state today.

The present owners, the Minton Group, plan to change the mill buildings into a restaurant. With the mill stream alongside, this could again be a very attractive area. One of the modern office buildings is to remain and continue in its original use, but the rest of the buildings from different decades would be demolished including Cowbridge House. With the very necessary, but extremely ugly, 1940s brick extension built onto the front of the House it now has little charm. Like so many country houses taken over as an emergency during the war years, it suffered and has continued to do so over the years. Whilst it would be a romantic dream to see it as it once was, that can never be. We live in a very different world. The plan is to build homes on the site; several of these would incorporate office space for the owners to work from home, a fast growing trend today.

What is almost certain is the fact that even if Cowbridge House is demolished, which is more than likely, its story and the story of the people who lived and worked in the house and factory will live on. The impact and influence it has had over the years on the town of Malmesbury will not change.